Samuel French Acting Edition

Porno Stars At Home
A Comedy-Drama

by Leonard Melfi

SAMUELFRENCH.COM   SAMUELFRENCH.CO.UK

Copyright © 1980 by Leonard Melfi
All Rights Reserved

PORNO STARS AT HOME is fully protected under the copyright laws of the United States of America, the British Commonwealth, including Canada, and all other countries of the Copyright Union. All rights, including professional and amateur stage productions, recitation, lecturing, public reading, motion picture, radio broadcasting, television and the rights of translation into foreign languages are strictly reserved.

ISBN 978-0-573-61446-0

www.SamuelFrench.com
www.SamuelFrench.co.uk

For Production Enquiries

United States and Canada
Info@SamuelFrench.com
1-866-598-8449

United Kingdom and Europe
Plays@SamuelFrench.co.uk
020-7255-4302

Each title is subject to availability from Samuel French, depending upon country of performance. Please be aware that *PORNO STARS AT HOME* may not be licensed by Samuel French in your territory. Professional and amateur producers should contact the nearest Samuel French office or licensing partner to verify availability.

CAUTION: Professional and amateur producers are hereby warned that *PORNO STARS AT HOME* is subject to a licensing fee. Publication of this play(s) does not imply availability for performance. Both amateurs and professionals considering a production are strongly advised to apply to Samuel French before starting rehearsals, advertising, or booking a theatre. A licensing fee must be paid whether the title(s) is presented for charity or gain and whether or not admission is charged. Professional/Stock licensing fees are quoted upon application to Samuel French.

No one shall make any changes in this title(s) for the purpose of production. No part of this book may be reproduced, stored in a retrieval system, or transmitted in any form, by any means, now known or yet to be invented, including mechanical, electronic, photocopying, recording, videotaping, or otherwise, without the prior written permission of the publisher. No one shall upload this title(s), or part of this title(s), to any social media websites.

For all enquiries regarding motion picture, television, and other media rights, please contact Samuel French.

Please refer to page 71 for further copyright information.

For:
JODY CATLIN
and
JUSTIN DEAS
(alphabetically)

CHESTER FOX & MARTIN J. AIN
present

PORNO STARS AT HOME

A New Comedy-Drama
By LEONARD MELFI
Directed by KEN EULO

Starring

ALAN BROOKS **JODY CATLIN** **JUSTIN DEAS**

TARA TYSON **MEG WITTNER**

Incidental music composed and played by

PHILIP ADELMAN

Setting by	*Costumes by*	*Lighting by*
ROBERT ANTHONY	**ANDY NAVARRE**	**SAM BUCCIO**

Set Co-Ordinator **ANTHONY RIZZO**

Production Stage Manager **MICCI TOLIVER**

PORNO STARS AT HOME was presented at the Courtyard Playhouse in New York City on November 28, 1978.

CAST

(In order of appearance)

GEORGIA LLOYD BERNHARDT	Tara Tyson
MUSICIAN	Philip Adelman
BARRY OLIVIER	Justin Deas
NORMA JEAN BRANDO	Jody Catlin
MONTGOMERY MCQUEEN	Alan Brooks
UTA BERGMAN-HAYES	Meg Wittner

NOTE: The first production of PORNO STARS AT HOME was also presented at the Courtyard Playhouse in New York City on January 28th, 1976, under Ken Eulo's direction with the following cast, in order of appearance:

GEORGIA LLOYD BERNHARDT	Rebecca Stanley
MUSICIAN	Philip Adelman
BARRY OLIVIER	Michael Lamont
NORMA JEAN BRANDO	Jody Catlin
MONTGOMERY MCQUEEN	Richard Hayes
UTA BERGMAN-HAYES	Grace Woodard

(The use of the MUSICIAN in the production of the play is completely optional.)

SYNOPSIS

The action of the play takes place in the New York apartment of Georgia Lloyd Bernhardt.

ACT ONE

Time: 9:00 P.M.

ACT TWO

Time: 2:25 A.M.

THE PEOPLE OF THE PLAY
(as they appear)

GEORGIA LLOYD BERNHARDT: she is about 35 and she is a good-looking blonde with a good-looking body, and it is quite obvious that she has taken various speech lessons; she is all dressed up in pure solid white: a long fluffy-white-type "gown" that goes down to her ankles with a slit on both sides that goes all the way up to her thighs: revealing a pair of beautifully-shaped legs; the "gown" is also intensely low-cut: revealing a pair of solid, round, grapefruit-shaped breasts; her skin is very white and very pale and very smooth, just like marble; she wears bloody-red lipstick, however, and bloody-red loop earrings and a number of bloody-red rings on her flickering white fingers; she also carries a bloody-red kerchief which she "plays around with" a whole lot; finally: she is a constant cigarette smoker and the cigarettes are always supported by a bloody-red cigarette holder.

BARRY OLIVIER: he is also about 35 and he is dark and handsome and thin and not quite six-feet; he has dark wild hair and a dark wild mustache to go with it; he has a Bronx accent and does nothing about it; he wears a bright yellow dress-shirt, a bright yellow necktie that matches the shirt, a pair of white Levi's which are brand-new, a gold chain for a belt and a gold chain around his neck which matches the belt, and, finally, a white leather-looking jacket which also has golden-looking buttons; he puffs on long thin cigars most of the time.

NORMA JEAN BRANDO: a real raven-haired beauty who is in her mid-20's and who looks even better looking when her dark rich full head of soft smooth hair is worn up like a tight tempting turban; she is built both sexually and delicately and her gardenia-shaded complexion looks simply terrific in contrast to her dark hair and dark eyes; when she walks and when she sits we are sometimes reminded of a dancer; she wears a perfect-fitting light baby-blue dress which is made of satin, white high heels, a white pearl necklace, and a big floppy white felt hat which almost gives her a high-fashion model image and which she keeps taking off and putting on; she also wears huge white-rimmed sunglasses which she also keeps taking off and then putting on.

MONTGOMERY MCQUEEN: he is a very "pretty-looking" guy in his early 20's; he has sandy blonde hair which makes us think of Prince Valiant and he is fairly thin but with good muscles; he gives a rather forced athletic impression and walks hard on his soles a whole lot; he wears a pair of tight clean denims with a thick black leather belt that has a gleaming gold buckle, a pair of expensive cowboy boots, tan-colored and with high heels since he is not very tall, a purple velvet shirt with bolero sleeves and which he keeps unbuttoned almost down to his waist, and, finally: a golden cross which dangles around his neck from a long leather neck-chain.

UTA BERGMAN-HAYES: she is close to 30 and she is lovely to look at except that she always tries to look plain and simple in "real-life"; her hair is a very dark reddish brown and she wears it rather neatly—almost like a halo—about her head; her skin is soft and smooth and very gentle-looking—the same as her voice and speech patterns—and she is built rather tiny: but it is all nicely put together; she wears a jet black pants suit which is very simple, black high heels, a white blouse made of lady-like silk, and an "emerald" necklace with earrings and a bracelet to match; she also carries a large bright green bag slung over her right shoulder, and sometimes over her left shoulder as well.

WHERE THEY ARE

GEORGIA LLOYD BERNHARDT's apartment: the living room. It is a ground-floor apartment, rather small, and the living room, which takes up all of the stage area, is quite unreal to behold: which is as it should be: everything is white: no matter where you look: except for bright green plants which seem to be everywhere: especially those that hang from the ceiling: they seem to make a roof of greenery: it reminds us of a tiny vineyard-type-place set up for a picnic and protected from the sun and the rain. The apartment is located somewhere in the West 70's, just off Central Park West in Manhattan.

WHEN

A night in February during the present time.

PORNO STARS AT HOME

ACT ONE

Before the lights come up on the stage area we hear a 1975 rock-vocal rendition of: "Could It Be I'm Falling In Love?" which is playing over the radio in GEORGIA LLOYD BERNHARDT'S *apartment. Finally, the lights go down in the theatre and the lights come up Onstage. The music is finished. The stage is empty. Another song begins to play. It is Olivia Newton-John singing: "Something Better To Do."* GEORGIA LLOYD BERNHARDT *enters the living room of her apartment in a hot red light; eventually, the hot red light goes away, while* GEORGIA *lights a brand new cigarette and pours herself a glass of rich red wine. She stands alone in the middle of the living room and lifts her wine glass up in a toasting gesture. She talks to herself: loud and clear: it is as though she is auditioning for a part of some kind.*

GEORGIA. Happy birthday, Georgia Lloyd Bernhardt, honey, and congratulations for getting the part of the unhappy frustrated suburban housewife living in such anxious agonized agony and in such dismaying disenchanted discouraging disillusioned disarray in some dull dismal disheartening suburb of some real typical hick town somewhere smack in the heart of America. (*She drinks.*) It's going to be such a wonderful challenge: playing a part like that: it's the total opposite of me: it's so wonderful tonight: to be me: and it's even more wonderful than I could ever have thought it could be: because it's also my birthday! (*She drinks again.*) I think it's going to be a very pleasant birthday party. People should give their own birthday parties because birthdays are such personally dramatic experiences. Birthday parties given by other people whose birthdays have arrived are for shit. *Surprise* birthday parties given by other people whose birthdays have arrived are even more for shit: they also suck! (*She drinks some more.*) I wonder what I should do: I wonder whether or not I should give my speech when they're all here together or whether I should give my speech when they arrive one at a time. (*In a rehearsed manner.*) We're all going to drink. I have the drink that each one of you drink: Jack Daniel's-on-the-rocks-with-a-twist-of-lemon for Barry the beautiful hairy Teddy-Bear; New York champagne for Norma Jean the beautiful raven-haired siren of the super-sexual-silver-sucking precious porno movie screen; Cutty Sark Scotch-with-milk-with-one-ice-cube for Montgomery the gorgeous gallantly giving extra-good Kid Galahad; and, finally: Smirnoff Vodka-screwdrivers-in-extra-tall-glasses for Uta the universal woman of some far-off united Utopia. You may all drink; you may all drink as much as you want. But no drugs, please! I don't allow the smoking of grass and the like in my house. And no coke, no hash, no heroin, no LSD, no mescaline, no morphine, and no poppers, and the like: not under my roof, if you please! (*She drinks again.*) And, finally, once again: no profanity allowed in my place, please: I don't want to hear anything that sounds in any way like: cunt and cunt-lapper, cock and cock-sucker, muff-diver and pussy and prick teaser, tits and balls and ass, dick and dork and wang, snatch and box and hole . . . and the like . . . and, of course: I especially do not want to hear the word *fuck* under any circumstances while anyone is present inside the various four walls of my warm and cozy apartment. (*She finishes the glass of wine. The door buzzer is heard; it buzzes once.* GEORGIA *"fixes" herself up in an "imagined" mirror. She pours herself another glass of red wine; she lights a new cigarette.*) Come in.

(BARRY OLIVIER *enters in a bright yellow light; eventually it disappears; music is heard in the background: The Captain and Tennielle singing: "The Way I Wanna Touch You."*)

BARRY. Wow! This is really some apartment. Wow! I mean I really like the design of it. The *decor:* I guess that's the right word. (*He totally ignores* GEORGIA, *but not intentionally, as he goes on his private little "inspection tour" of* GEORGIA's *living room.*) *Decor!* Wow! It makes me hate my place. My place is a real hole-in-the-wall. It's dark and dank and damp and dreary and dung-smelling. But I guess that's because I got my pet monkey living with me. His name is Barry The Second, after me, naturally, and he won't go out and shit; he'll only shit in my pad . . . (GEORGIA *is making* BARRY *his drink.*)

GEORGIA. Defecate, darling.

BARRY. What . . . ?

GEORGIA. The word is defecate, darling. I don't allow dirty words in the place where I live. (*She hands him his drink.*)

BARRY. How are you, Georgia?! And Happy Birthday, baby!

GEORGIA. Thanks.

BARRY. (*He kisses her on the lips as he shakes her hand.*) I think it's really terrific that you're having this birthday party for yourself.

GEORGIA. I think it's terrific that I am too.

BARRY. Here's your present. (BARRY *takes a tiny little box out of one of his pockets and gives it to her.*)

GEORGIA. Oh, thank you very much, Barry. (*She places it on a table.*)

BARRY. Aren't you going to open it now?

GEORGIA. We've got all night.

BARRY. What do you think?

GEORGIA. About what?

BARRY. Do you think it's going to be a good night?

GEORGIA. Why do you ask that?

BARRY. Because I want it to be a good night, that's why. I'm about ready for a good night. Things have been pretty depressing for me lately, if you know what I mean.

GEORGIA. First of all, let me tell you something.

BARRY. I'm all ears. And cock.

GEORGIA. I told you: *no* profanity in my house!

BARRY. I'm sorry. I'm all penis then.

GEORGIA. That's better. Now, as I was saying before: let me tell you something, darling. I think that the reason things have been pretty depressing for you lately is pretty plain and pretty simple. It's that pet monkey you got and the name that you've given him. Barry The Second! Why that's simply awful, darling! It's downright masochistic!

BARRY. I never thought of it that way.

GEORGIA. Why did you ever do such a self-destructive thing?

BARRY. I don't know . . .

GEORGIA. Naming a monkey after yourself! That *is* depressing! And having a monkey for a pet in the first place! Well, that's just as depressing too! What's the matter with you?! I've always thought that you were so different from the rest of us. I've always loved believing that you were the healthiest one of us all. I've always enjoyed thinking that you were the happiest one of all of us.

BARRY. But I am, I am!

GEORGIA. Well then get rid of that pet monkey of yours. You don't need a Barry The Second, at least not that sort of Barry The Second. You should give him away as soon as possible.

BARRY. I will, I will!

GEORGIA. Get yourself a nice cat instead.

BARRY. I don't like cats. They turn me off. You can't play with cats the way you can play with dogs. You can't pet cats the way you can pet dogs. You can't hold cats the way you can hold dogs. Cats never lick your hands the way that dogs lick your hands. Cats are like broads. Dogs are like guys. It's easy to be friends with guys but it's so hard to be friends with broads. I've always thought of all cats as being broads, and I've always thought of all dogs as being guys. Cats are like broads because they give the impression of being way ahead of you. They make you think they know more than you do. Jesus Christ: but it would be just a real down trip if I had a cat: my ego would be absolutely nowhere if I had a cat!

GEORGIA. Then get yourself a goddam dog, for Christ's sake!

BARRY. I think that's a good idea.

GEORGIA. You know, Barry darling, I'm really beginning to wonder about you now.

BARRY. What are you beginning to wonder about?

GEORGIA. About what I thought about you before. Are you the healthiest? Are you the happiest? I don't want to feel sad all of a sudden just because I think I might be disappointed all of a sudden.

BARRY. I don't want you to be sad and I don't want you to be disappointed, Georgia. There's no way that you're going to lay that trip on me. I am the healthiest! And I am the happiest!

GEORGIA. Then don't let me down: prove it. Right now!

BARRY. I'm the healthiest and I'm the happiest because I'm able to say what I just said to you: about the difference between dogs and cats, and about my ego. You know what I mean? I mean I can talk about it to people. I can face anything on my own, Georgia. I am the healthiest and I am the happiest. I enjoy having sex before those cameras, and I enjoy sex when I'm not before those cameras. Sex on the screen and sex off the screen are both the same for me: I love it all! And I'm straight, baby, too. I mean, well, let me tell you what I mean: I mean I'm the healthiest and I'm the happiest because I've done everything at least once, I've tried everything at least twice, because I really and truly believe in that, doing just that, because in the end, well, you finally find out together you are, I mean, that is, if you don't hold back and you discover everything, and then you wind up making all of the choices that you feel are best for you. You were right in the first place, Georgia Lloyd Bernhardt: I am the healthiest and the happiest because I've done all of this and I've also been able to talk to you about it. And I've got this steady broad too, and she's the perfect girlfriend for a guy like me to have, her name is Lorna Lou and she reminds me of a younger version of you, and she listens to me just the way you've been listening to me, and we been seeing each other for over a year now . . . and just last month we finally got engaged. I bought her a terrific-looking engagement ring on 47th Street, and she was with me when I bought it, and it turned out to be the best afternoon of our lives so far. I'm the healthiest and the happiest because I'm also doing everything the way everything is really supposed to be done, if you know what I mean. Do you know what I mean, Georgia? (GEORGIA *finishes her wine.*)

GEORGIA. You know something? You're good to have around the house.

BARRY. That's nice of you.

GEORGIA. Don't mention it.

BARRY. How about another drink?

GEORGIA. You're on your own after the first which means you help yourself from now on and which also means that you can have all you want because I've got lots more in the closet.

BARRY. (*Makes himself another drink.*) So who else is coming?

GEORGIA. The remaining three. I mean the other three best ones in America besides you and I. At least that's what I think: it's my expert pornographic opinion: there's you and me and Norma Jean and Montgomery and Uta, and that's it, there ain't no more as far as I'm concerned.

BARRY. I'll tell you something: coming from you: well, that's a compliment.

GEORGIA. Of course it is.

BARRY. It's almost too hard to believe in the confidence that you have. But I suppose it's only right: the fact that you should have such terrific confidence. You're the original, when you really come right down to it.

GEORGIA. So very true, darling. But you're the original too: the male version, of course.

BARRY. Of course.

GEORGIA. I've got a lovely secret, Barry.

BARRY. Honest?

GEORGIA. Honest.

BARRY. Do you want to tell me what it is?

GEORGIA. Oh, but of course I do. But I'm going to wait. I'm going to wait until everybody else is here. Then I'll tell my secret.

BARRY. Will I like it?

GEORGIA. Well, I want you to like it. But I'm a little afraid: I'm a little afraid that you all might get a little jealous, and if that's the case, well, it might ruin my birthday party.

BARRY. None of us would want to do that.

GEORGIA. I want to believe you when you say that. I hope you're right.

BARRY. *(After a pause.)* Do you know what I was just thinking? I was just thinking about the two of us: about what we do before the cameras together.

GEORGIA. I try never to think about it, darling.

BARRY. I'm thinking about the fact that we never get it off together offscreen. I mean: we've never even made an attempt at getting it off together in real life in your apartment or my apartment or in some hotel room somewhere. I guess I've been thinking about that a whole lot because it's got me sort of confused, and, well, I really think it might be a real trip if we made an attempt at it sometime. (*A pause.*) By the way, Georgia, I mean talking about having a secret. Well, I've got one too. You wanna know what it is?

GEORGIA. Not if it's going to make me jealous the way I think that my secret might make the rest of you jealous.

BARRY. I don't think it'll make you jealous. But I do think that it'll make you think.

GEORGIA. I'm not up to thinking too much tonight.

BARRY. I guess tonight's really going to be the night . . .

GEORGIA. The night for what?

BARRY. The night for no thinking. The night for just relaxing. And nothing more.

GEORGIA. That's the way I hope the night's going to be.

BARRY. How about a little kiss on the lips before the rest of them come?

GEORGIA. Forget it.

BARRY. C'mon.

GEORGIA. No way.

BARRY. C'mon.

GEORGIA. We kissed on the lips when you first came in. When it's time for you to leave then we'll kiss on the lips again: it'll be a nice warm kiss-on-the-lips-good-night.

BARRY. But why can't it be more?

GEORGIA. Because I'm not into it, that's why.

BARRY. Is that the only reason why?

GEORGIA. Yes, that's the only reason why!

BARRY. Are you getting mad at me?

GEORGIA. Not yet.

BARRY. But you think that you could?

GEORGIA. Yes: I think that I could.

BARRY. Listen: after it gets pretty late and when the other three of them think that it's about time that they left, well, I'll pretend that I fell asleep, see? Fast asleep on the floor here because I'm so tired and so relaxed and so drunk from gallons of Jack Daniel's and hundreds of ice-cubes and kilos of lemon peels. You'll look down at me, see? And then you'll bend down and kneel over my sleeping body and you'll move my head very gently so that my sleeping face is facing you, and facing them too, and you'll make some comment about me being Barry the beautiful hairy Teddy-Bear, and that maybe it would be a good idea if you all just left me alone because I'm really just like a little boy-baby who fell asleep way past his normal bedtime and so it would be a terrible shame to wake me up then, especially since I really needed the sleep in the first place because I had to get up at seven o'clock in the morning in order to be at school on time at eight o'clock in the morning.

GEORGIA. Enough is enough!

BARRY. And so they'll listen to you which means that they'll all leave together, and then, just as soon as they're all gone: I'll jump up from the floor and carry you to your bedroom . . .

GEORGIA. I told you: enough is enough!

BARRY. Or better yet . . . (BARRY *throws himself down on the floor and lies on his back: looking up at* GEORGIA.)

GEORGIA. Get back up!

BARRY. I'll just stay lying down on my back like this and . . .

GEORGIA. I told you to get back up, darling!

BARRY. And you'll come down to the floor with me and . . .

GEORGIA. Will you listen to me?! Goddam you! You're just acting now, that's all you're doing!

BARRY. (*Sitting up.*) I am not!

GEORGIA. You are too! You're acting out all of your problems at my expense, that's what you're doing!

BARRY. (*Lying back down.*) That's not true!

GEORGIA. It is too!

BARRY. (*Still lying on his back.*) You'll come down here and you'll mount me, you'll straddle me . . .

GEORGIA. You're going to ruin my birthday party, Barry!

So get up! And stop all of this! Please?! It would never work, and you know it!

BARRY. (*Sitting up again.*) Don't be so negative.

GEORGIA. I'm never negative, goddam you! I hate it when people tell me that I'm negative! Goddam you! I'm the most positive person you'll ever meet in your whole goddam life, darling! And don't you forget it, either! You understand?! Goddam you!

BARRY. (*Still sitting up.*) Why are you getting so mad, Georgia?

GEORGIA. Because you're just as freaked out as I am, that's why! I look at you down there and I listen to your mouth from down there and it just simply makes me think of myself, and you, and just simply how freaked out you are and how freaked out I am. The two of us! So get up, goddam you! Get up so that we can get back into our original mood! Otherwise: this birthday party is going to be a disaster! You don't want that to happen, do you?! I know you don't. And I don't, either. I've been married five times, you know that. And I'm in the process of getting my fifth divorce: you know that, too. I've had five husbands and no children. I've had seven miscarriages. That's why I have no children. You know that, too. So get up right now, this very second, please?! You're not going to freak me out any further than I'm already freaked out! Do you understand?! Get up right now this very second so that you don't freak yourself out any further, either! Goddam you! (*There is a pause.* BARRY *looks up at* GEORGIA.)

BARRY. You really mean it, don't you . . . ?

GEORGIA. Yes, I really do . . . (BARRY *gets up from the floor.*)

BARRY. All right for you, Georgia . . .

GEORGIA. You're still a darling.

BARRY. Okay then.

GEORGIA. I really appreciate your listening to me the way you just did.

BARRY. I said: okay then. (BARRY *goes and pours more Jack Daniel's into his glass.*)

GEORGIA. A disaster is a disaster is a disaster. We don't want a disaster tonight simply because we don't need a disaster tonight. We don't want a disaster, we don't need a disaster any night or any day or any time. My birthday party is not going to be a disaster tonight. (*A pause.*) Maybe someday, Barry, maybe someday, a day in the near future, perhaps, well, maybe that future day in the not-too-distant future will finally lead into the nighttime of that very same special day: and it will be the right time . . . *maybe* . . . for you and for me, and if it is, well, you can be certain that it won't be a disaster . . . ! (BARRY *turns to face* GEORGIA *with a bright twinkle in his eyes.*)

BARRY. You know something?
GEORGIA. What?
BARRY. You're so positive!

(GEORGIA *feels so much better now; they both give long warm smiles to each other. The door buzzer rings: two short buzzes.*)

GEORGIA. Well, it's about time.
BARRY. Am I as positive as you are, Georgia?
GEORGIA. Almost. But that's because you're just a bit younger, that's all. (*The door buzzer rings again: the same two short buzzes.*) Come in. Whoever you are.
BARRY. Who do you think it is?
GEORGIA. Let's guess.
BARRY. It's Norma Jean Brando.
GEORGIA. I was going to guess her too. Isn't that funny?

(NORMA JEAN BRANDO *enters in a baby-blue-hued light which slowly dies away. We hear music by Chicago:* "*Saturday In The Park.*")

NORMA JEAN. Hello, Georgia. Hello, Barry. I love your place, Georgia. I love your outfit, Barry. I love yours, too, Georgia . . . I really do. It's true. I'm not just saying it. I'm saying it because I mean it. I'm telling you the truth: both of you. Oh, God: your place is so interesting, Georgia. I loved coming here tonight because I loved thinking what an interesting birthday party it's probably going to be tonight. (NORMA JEAN *goes and gives* GEORGIA *a kiss and a hug.*) We're all such interesting people in real life which is so frustrating and so nerve-racking because I have this awfully funny and awfully sad feeling that the general moviegoing public at large think that we're all really dull and dreary and just plain uninteresting. But of course they're all wrong and really just don't know any better. (NORMA JEAN *goes and gives* BARRY *a kiss and a hug now.*) I love your cigarette holder, Georgia. I love the smell of your cigar smoke, Barry. I love the idea of giving your own birthday party. It says something nice: it says that you really love yourself, Georgia. I love that. I also love the fact that you came here before I did, Barry. Do you know why? Well, I'll tell you both why: because I've always felt that you, Georgia, and you, Barry, should really and truly get together, get it on together, and get it off together, I really and truly mean it, you two. I'm not playing Cupid or anything like that, and I'm certainly not a matchmaker of any kind, but it's always been on my mind, and I've always secretly wished it: the two of you getting together. I live vicariously lots of times, most of the time I find myself living vicariously, just simply through my fantasies of the people who I think should be together. I love couplings and I really love coupling certain people. I just simply love vicarious thoughts, but I would be even happier if the thoughts that I love so much would no longer be vicarious. I would love that most of all. I need a drink fast! (GEORGIA *goes and makes* NORMA JEAN *her drink.*) Oh, my God, Georgia! I forgot to wish you: Happy Birthday! Happy Birthday,

Georgia sweetheart! I love you! I hope this is your best birthday ever! I hope that we can all be as super-terrific as you are when we get to be your age! I mean that, of course, as a super-supreme, not-so-sublime compliment: I mean it from the bottom of my non-pornographic heart and from the deepest part of my extreme, ultra, nonpornographic soul. Shit, goddammit, shit! Why am I sounding so goddam guilty about being a porno star? A *super* porno star?! (GEORGIA *gives a drink to* NORMA JEAN.) Thank you very much, sweetheart. (NORMA JEAN *lifts her drink.*) To you, Georgia Lloyd Bernhardt, on your birthday! I hope you're as happy as I am just being here. And thank you so much for feeling that you wanted to invite me in the first place. I really love that! It makes me terribly happy: just the mere fact of that alone. Happy Birthday, Georgia! (NORMA JEAN *takes a long sip of her drink.*)

GEORGIA. Well, now: thank you too.

NORMA JEAN. You have such a marvelous memory, Georgia: remembering my drink the way you have. I wish I could be that way. Maybe it'll rub off on me from you. I would love that a whole lot.

GEORGIA. Well, thank you, again. Listen, darling, I hate to bring this up. But I think I'd better right now: I don't allow profanity under my roof where I live.

NORMA JEAN. Was I using profanity?

GEORGIA. Yes, you were . . .

BARRY. You said "shit" twice and "goddammit" once . . .

GEORGIA. Barry's right . . .

NORMA JEAN. I did? Well, I don't even remember I did. But, no matter: I'll do my best to keep on my non-profanitied toes from here on in. Is Montgomery coming? I mean I should have said: is MM coming?

GEORGIA. As far as I know: MM is coming. I certainly hope he does, anyway.

BARRY. He doesn't want to be called MM anymore.

NORMA JEAN. Since when?

BARRY. Since the other day. He told me he's uncomfortable with it now. He wants to be known on his own. He wants to be known for himself.

GEORGIA. He's growing up, isn't he?

NORMA JEAN. I love him. The way I love the two of you. (NORMA JEAN *finishes her drink.*)

GEORGIA. From now on: you're on your own, Norma Jean.

NORMA JEAN. What does that mean?

BARRY. It means you make all of your own drinks from now on . . .

NORMA JEAN. Oh . . . ?

GEORGIA. Which means that my place is your place for the rest of this birthday evening in little ole' New York.

NORMA JEAN. That's lovely. (NORMA JEAN *goes to make herself another drink.*)

BARRY. And don't worry, either, Norma Jean.

NORMA JEAN. Worry?

BARRY. Don't worry about running out of champagne . . .

GEORGIA. Champagne from New York, of course . . .

BARRY. Georgia has a closet just filled with it.

NORMA JEAN. I'm so grateful. It's the only kind of champagne that I like: New York champagne. After all, we are living in very modern times. New York champagne just sounds so much more right to me these days than French champagne. I was never really one for dealing with the past, you see: always the present, you see?! New York champagne is perfectly right for me! (*The door buzzer rings three long distinct buzzes.*)

GEORGIA. Shall we guess again, Barry?

BARRY. I think it's . . .

NORMA JEAN. MM! I mean it's Montgomery McQueen!

GEORGIA. I was going to guess the same thing . . .

BARRY. So was I.

NORMA JEAN. This is so much fun already. Do you have milk for him, Georgia? I know you have the Cutty Sark.

GEORGIA. Gallons, darling.

NORMA JEAN. I just can't believe how your memory is, Georgia. Maybe you can help me with that too. It always scares me, which, of course, is just really, simply awful when you truly think about the mere fact that I'm such a very serious and very dedicated actress in the end. (*The door buzzer is heard again: three long distinct buzzes again.*)

GEORGIA. Come in. Whoever you are.

(MONTGOMERY MCQUEEN *enters in a deep purple light which slowly fades away in the air. We hear Laura Nyro singing "The Wedding Bell Blues." He carries a huge green plant that has large blood-red buds in a bright red flower pot.* GEORGIA, BARRY, *and* NORMA JEAN *all stop and stare at him; nobody says a thing; it is as though they are all making a silent tribute to youth; it is both reverent and very touching and rather sad in a very nostalgic way;* MONTGOMERY *freezes in his tracks, and so do* GEORGIA, BARRY, *and* NORMA JEAN. *Eventually,* MONTGOMERY *begins to sing to* GEORGIA *above the music of "The Wedding Bell Blues" and the voice of Laura Nyro.*)

MONTGOMERY. (*Singing.*) Happy birthday to you, Happy Birthday to you, Happy Birthday, dear Georgia, Happy Birthday to you. (*They all laugh rather nicely together.* MONTGOMERY *gives the plant to* GEORGIA.)

GEORGIA. Oh, Montgomery, thank you, *thank you!* (GEORGIA *gives him a light kiss on the lips.* MONTGOMERY *goes and kisses* NORMA JEAN *on the lips; they hug each other rather desperately.*)

NORMA JEAN. Oh, MM! I'm sorry! I mean my dear

Montgomery McQueen: I love you! Montgomery McQueen! I love you!

MONTGOMERY. The feeling's mutual, Norma Jean The Ultimate Supreme! (BARRY *goes to* MONTGOMERY *and shakes his hand.* MONTGOMERY *hugs* BARRY *and then they kiss on the lips too.*)

BARRY. I love you, baby!

MONTGOMERY. The same goes here, baby Barry. (MONTGOMERY *moves away from all of them now: he looks directly at* GEORGIA.) I forgot, Georgia. I forgot how old you are.

GEORGIA. So did I. (*They all smile and giggle and laugh a little.*)

MONTGOMERY. I think it's thirty-five, even if you look twenty-five.

GEORGIA. You're right, darling: it's thirty-five. But thank you for thinking I look twenty-five: you wanna know something? I believe you. (GEORGIA *blows him a long "wet" kiss.* MONTGOMERY *begins to sing again; he sings to* GEORGIA.)

MONTGOMERY and NORMA JEAN. (*Singing.*) Thirty-five *pink* candles we will take, Put them on a birthday cake, All for Georgia: holy sakes, Georgia's thirty-five years old!

(*They all applaud and laugh joyously as* GEORGIA *goes and gives* MONTGOMERY *a bigger kiss than ever before. The door buzzer is heard again: four short distinct buzzes; "The Wedding Bell Blues" sung by Laura Nyro is still playing in the background.*)

GEORGIA. We can't guess this time . . .
BARRY. It's Uta Bergman-Hayes . . .
NORMA JEAN. I love her so much!
GEORGIA. Come in. We *know* who you are!

(UTA BERGMAN-HAYES *enters in a beaming emerald-green light which eventually envelopes itself into the immediate atmosphere; "The Wedding Bell Blues" being sung by Laura Nyro gets louder than it ever was before.*)

UTA. (*To* GEORGIA.) Hello, Georgia. Happy birthday. Hello, Barry. Hello, Norma Jean. Hello, Montgomery.

GEORGIA. Hello, Uta. Thank you.

BARRY. Hello, Uta.

NORMA JEAN. Hello, Uta. I just love you so much!

MONTGOMERY. Hello, Uta. How you doin'?

UTA. I'm okay . . . I guess . . . Montgomery. (*So far:* UTA *has not made one attempt at touching any of them physically; it is also sort of obvious.*)

GEORGIA. I want to hug you, darling. (GEORGIA *goes to* UTA *and gives her a big warm hug;* UTA *"gives in" a little bit.*)

UTA. I'm sorry . . . Georgia . . .

GEORGIA. After all: it *is* my birthday: it's a time for celebrating as much as possible, darling.

UTA. I think I agree . . . with you, Georgia. (GEORGIA *turns to face them all now. She looks at* MONTGOMERY.)

MONTGOMERY. (*Smiling most affectionately.*) Hi. Happy birthday again, Miss Georgia.

GEORGIA. Oh, dear! I nearly forgot, Montgomery: your drink! And you, Uta: your drink too! (GEORGIA *goes and begins to make them both their particular drinks.*)

UTA. If you don't have vodka, well, it's okay: I'll settle for gin, Georgia . . .

GEORGIA. No way . . .

BARRY. (*To* UTA.) Georgia's got a closetful of vodka for you, Uta.

UTA. That's very nice. But if you don't have grapefruit juice, well, orange juice will do, Georgia.

GEORGIA. I've got buckets of pure fresh grapefruit juice too, darling. (*To* MONTGOMERY.) And I've got a whole live lovely cow in the kitchen: just for you, darling, just in case we run out of fresh pure white wholesome milk for you and your Cutty-Sark-Scotch-with-one-ice-cube.
NORMA JEAN. I'm really jealous of you, Georgia!
GEORGIA. Stop it, dear.
NORMA JEAN. Oh, no! I mean: jealous in a good way, a very positive way, sweetheart. I'm jealous of you because I think that you can love people even more than I thought I could love them, that's what I really meant. (GEORGIA *hands a drink to* UTA.)
UTA. Thank you, Georgia.
BARRY. All right, Georgia: now that we're all here: tell us your secret.
NORMA JEAN. Georgia's got a secret? How interesting.

(GEORGIA *hands a drink to* MONTGOMERY. UTA *and* MONTGOMERY *both lift their glasses in the air in the direction of* GEORGIA.)

UTA. Happy birthday . . .
MONTGOMERY. Happy birthday . . . ! (UTA *and* MONTGOMERY *both drink their drinks.*)
NORMA JEAN. I love secrets! And I love you, Barry, for letting us in on the fact that Georgia has a secret. And, of course, Georgia, I love you most of all, at the moment, that is, for having a secret in the first place: in order to tell us all what it is, in the first place!
BARRY. (*To* NORMA JEAN.) Do you ever stop!
NORMA JEAN. You talking to me?
GEORGIA. Darling: you haven't *stopped* since you came. (NORMA JEAN *is just a bit embarrassed perhaps.*)
NORMA JEAN. Well, I guess that's why I haven't stopped: I mean to say: ever since the first time that *I came:* well, I just haven't ever been able to stop!

GEORGIA. Forget we even mentioned it.
BARRY. (*To* GEORGIA.) The secret, Georgia?
GEORGIA. In a little while . . .
UTA. Oh, I forgot, Georgia . . .
GEORGIA. What . . . ?
UTA. Your birthday present. It's in my bag here. (UTA *begins to open her large bag.*)
NORMA JEAN. My birthday gift is not real: I mean it's not something that I bought for you, Georgia.
GEORGIA. Oh . . . ?
UTA. Here you are, Georgia. (UTA *hands* GEORGIA *a small, beautifully-wrapped birthday gift.*)
GEORGIA. Thank you very much, darling.
UTA. You're welcome.
BARRY. Georgia, when are you going to tell us the secret?
GEORGIA. When I bring out the birthday cake and after I blow out all of my candles and after I cut into the birthday cake and after we all dig into it: that's when I'm gonna open up my birthday gifts, darling-Hairy-beautiful-Barry-little-boy-wonder!
BARRY. Aw, shit!
GEORGIA. All right, all right! I'll open up my birthday presents just before my birthday cake. And I told you not to use profanity in my house.
BARRY. Hey, that's right, Montgomery; that's right, Uta: Georgia doesn't dig any dirty words under her roof.
UTA. I can go along with that.
NORMA JEAN. It's awfully difficult, but so far I've been doing pretty well, don't you think?
GEORGIA. Terrific.
NORMA JEAN. Do you know something? My birthday gift to you, in a way, is also a secret. I mean it's something I'm going to tell you, Georgia. It's something for all of us, really.
BARRY. Will it make us all happy?
NORMA JEAN. Oh, yes! By all means! The five of us will

be overjoyed! Actually, I'm already overjoyed because I know what it already is!

MONTGOMERY. I need another drink . . .

UTA. So do I.

BARRY. You're on your own then. Georgia's house rules. You both just help yourselves from now on, right, Georgia?

GEORGIA. Yes, Barry. Right, Barry. (MONTGOMERY *and* UTA *both go together to make their individual drinks together.* GEORGIA *looking at the plant that* MONTGOMERY *brought her.*) It's just beautiful, that's all I can say, Montgomery, just simply beautiful.

MONTGOMERY. Well, it's about time, Georgia.

GEORGIA. What does that mean, darling?

MONTGOMERY. Well, it's about time you noticed my birthday present to you; it's about time you finally recognized the plant that I went out and bought especially for you.

GEORGIA. But darling Montgomery: I was so enthralled by your entrance: singing "happy birthday" the way you were singing it to me when you first came in: and then singing that unusual little "pink candle" melody for me right afterwards the way you did, well, darling, I'm sorry, but I just simply had to come down to the good hard solid earth again before I could even deal with this exotic, this exquisite, this extremely extra-enticing extra-engrossing extra-enervating deep green and bright blood-red birthday plant that you bought for me especially, and that you brought to me especially. I'm really sorry, darling Montgomery. I was intoxicated and overwhelmed beyond all words, that's all.

BARRY. (*To* MONTGOMERY.) She really means all of that too . . .

NORMA JEAN. I wish that I could have expressed it that way.

GEORGIA. Oh, honey! You could have done a whole lot better, believe me, if you just had the right opportunity, believe me.

MONTGOMERY. I was only joking with you, Georgia: honest-to-God I was.

GEORGIA. I'm sure you actually were. But, no matter, I did need to feel a little guilty about it, darling.

MONTGOMERY. It's a heart-and-soul plant, Georgia.

GEORGIA. A heart-and-soul plant? I love it even more than I thought I could love it.

UTA. It sounds lovely, doesn't it?

MONTGOMERY. The bright blood-red buds, just ready to burst open any second now, well, they represent your bright blood-red heart, Georgia. There are eight of them, see . . . ?

GEORGIA. (*Counting the buds.*) One, two, three, four . . .

MONTGOMERY. Well, today you're thirty-five, right . . . ?

(*They have all gathered around the plant now: almost as though it were a newly-decorated Christmas tree on Christmas Eve.*)

GEORGIA. (*Still counting.*) Five, six, seven . . .

MONTGOMERY. And the combination of three-and-eight out of thirty-five adds up to the number eight, and you're always telling all of us how eight has always been your lucky number ever since you could remember, right? And so, the lucky number of eight for you, Georgia, also represents eight very lucky parts of your bright blood-red heart, which really means that you've got more heart than anybody else, which means that you're all heart, which also means that you've got so much of your personal bright blood-red heart to go around with that you can easily allow it to be in eight separate parts: eight lovely individual parts all connected together and all growing together at the same time, you see? (GEORGIA *is enthralled;* BARRY *is listening intently;* NORMA JEAN *is delighted; and* UTA, *at this point, never takes her eyes off of* MONTGOMERY: *she clings to every word he says.*) And now we come to the soul of the plant: *your* soul, Georgia. The soul of this very rare and very special, deep green, bright blood-red, heart-and-soul birthday plant is represented by all of the deep green leaves and the rich lush stems and delicate deep green branches, which means, Georgia Lloyd Bernhardt, that your soul is everywhere in every place at every time, which, in turn, means that your soul is giving and spreading and unselfish and selfless and kind and generous, which finally means that the four of us here at your birthday party are the luckiest people in the entire world at the moment simply because of the lovely and lucky likes of you, *and only you!* Amen!

UTA. I . . . just . . . can't . . . believe . . . it . . . ! (UTA *faints on the floor.*)

GEORGIA. Oh, dear!

NORMA JEAN. What happened to her?!

BARRY. She fainted! (BARRY *and* MONTGOMERY *go to the aid of* UTA.)

MONTGOMERY. I wonder what's wrong with her! (BARRY *and* MONTGOMERY *help each other by helping* UTA *up from the floor. They carry her to the sofa and place her on it very gently.*)

GEORGIA. She's been so delicate these days . . .

NORMA JEAN. I've seen that too . . .

BARRY. She's not too happy these days . . .

MONTGOMERY. I've noticed that too . . . (GEORGIA *and* NORMA JEAN *gather around the sofa along with* BARRY *and* MONTGOMERY.)

GEORGIA. Uta . . . ?

NORMA JEAN. Uta . . . ?

BARRY. Uta . . . ? (MONTGOMERY *leans over and whispers very tenderly in* UTA*'s ear.*)

MONTGOMERY. Uta . . . ? Are you all right now, Uta . . . ? Is everything okay . . . ? Can you hear me, Uta . . . ? (UTA *begins to move a bit.*)

UTA. (*Whispering.*) Who . . . is . . . it . . . ?

GEORGIA. It's all of us, darling.

NORMA JEAN. It's me, sweetheart.

BARRY. We're all here, baby.

MONTGOMERY. *(Whispering in* UTA's *other ear now.)* Uta . . . ?

UTA. Who is it . . . ?

MONTGOMERY. It's me: Montgomery McQueen. (UTA *finally opens her eyes.)*

UTA. I'm so glad . . . it's *you!*

GEORGIA. *(Quietly.* What does that mean?

UTA. You were so wonderful . . . !

NORMA JEAN. *(Not so quietly.)* She's only into *him!*

UTA. I couldn't believe my ears, Montgomery . . . !

BARRY. *(To* NORMA JEAN.) Not so loud. This looks like a very serious thing to me . . .

UTA. And now I can hardly believe my eyes . . .

BARRY. You see? It is *very* serious. (UTA *begins to sit up with the aid of* MONTGOMERY *alone now.)*

MONTGOMERY. You okay, Uta?

UTA. *(Sitting up on the sofa.)* Oh, I'm just fine, now: thanks to you. Your story of the deep green and the bright blood-red birthday plant for Georgia was just too overwhelming for me, especially at this time in my life. It made me faint, and I'm sorry, but my fainting was really a token of my deepest appreciation for your intensely luscious eloquence all of a sudden like that. It just simply took me by complete surprise! (UTA *gets up from the sofa.)*

MONTGOMERY. Where you going?

UTA. I'm making myself another drink for myself. (UTA *goes and begins to make a new drink.)*

MONTGOMERY. I would have done it for you.

UTA. I believe you.

GEORGIA. *(Quietly.)* Christ. I'm beginning to feel like Mother Cupid on my birthday.

NORMA JEAN. Love's in sheer bloom!

BARRY. Yeah, man!

UTA. *(Taking a long swig of her new drink.)* Now I'm embarrassed!

GEORGIA. You shouldn't be.

NORMA JEAN. I wish I could be going what you're going through right now.

BARRY. There may be hope in the world after all.

UTA. Stop it! All of you! Except *you*, Montgomery . . . ! You're all seeing what you all would like to see; you're all hearing what you would all like to hear. Well, it's not true! I'm not interested in love because that means in the end I'm going to be forced to be interested in sex too. And you all know how I hate sex! On-screen and off-screen: well, I just despise it! You all know what an expert faker I am. You've all remarked to me at one time or another how you all wish you could be as successful as I am when it comes to faking it all. God only knows: I would like to enjoy it in my real life off-screen, but it just seems so utterly impossible now. Do you know why I do all those token dyke scenes in all of those hetero flicks? I do them because I can fake them better than the two of you ever could fake them, or anybody else for that matter!

GEORGIA. I don't do them because they turn me off.

UTA. Be quiet and let me finish . . .

NORMA JEAN. I don't do them for the same reason that Georgia just gave . . .

UTA. Shut up, Norma Jean!

NORMA JEAN. Sorry . . .

UTA. I loathe my robot attitude towards all of this. I don't want to be like a robot just because I'm really a human being like the rest of you. (UTA *finishes her second drink in one fast gulp.*) You see what two drinks will do to someone like me?! I've been to a hypnotist three times . . .

NORMA JEAN. Oh! I've always wanted to go to a hypnotist!

UTA. Shut up! And he was nowhere, the hypnotist! He told me to lie down on this water bed in his apartment somewhere near Carnegie Hall, and so I did what he told me. The first two times he controlled himself, but on the third visit the bastard tried to rape me! He turned out to be a goddam bullshit artist full of plain rotten shit at twenty-five bucks an hour! I could have killed him with my bare hands I was so mad!

GEORGIA. You can talk all you want, Uta, but would you please watch your language under my roof?

UTA. Oh, fuck your roof, Georgia!

GEORGIA. What . . . ?! (GEORGIA *begins to move towards* UTA.)

BARRY. Relax, Georgia. She doesn't mean anything personal.

UTA. I'm sorry, Georgia. I think the world of you. I would never want to hurt you, or any of you. I mean it! I just think playing all of those token Lesbian scenes is really getting to me lately, that's all. I'm not a dyke! But that's the whole trouble, I guess: I'm not anything!

GEORGIA. That's not true: *you're* everything!

NORMA JEAN. Georgia's right, Uta!

UTA. You girls are always so nice. I'm so grateful for that.

BARRY. Hey, we're all on edge because we ain't doing what we want to be doing, that's where it's really at. I studied for five years. I got in the studio after my second audition. Georgia's been studying longer than all of us . . . put together . . . !

GEORGIA. Yeah. Even voice.

NORMA JEAN. We're always making rounds, the five of us, and nothing happens. But that's where my secret birthday present to Georgia comes in: it's really a secret birthday present for all of us.

BARRY. Why don't you tell us what it is *now?!*

NORMA JEAN. Because Georgia wants me to wait until she opens her other birthday presents.

GEORGIA. My secret might not make the rest of you too happy. I hope I'm wrong.

UTA. (*Moving down towards* MONTGOMERY.) I'm sorry if I'm upsetting you, Montgomery.

MONTGOMERY. You're not really upsetting me: it's just

that I'm relating to you so much right now; I'm identifying with you completely right now. I don't feel very good about myself, either, you know? I mean: how would all of you want to be the superstar of all the gay movies with all-male casts for all-male audiences?! Especially since in real life: you're *not* gay at all! I'm *not* gay, I swear to God, I'm not! I've never told any of you this before but in my real personal life I can't get it up with a guy! I'm serious! My cock—sorry, Georgia—I mean my penis . . . my penis is like a long limp soft lumpy pudgy drooping pink marshmallow in real life whenever I've tried to do with men what I can do so well before the cameras. I have never been to bed with a man in real life successfully! Do you all understand that?! What I'm trying to say to all of you?!

GEORGIA. We understand . . .

NORMA JEAN. This is such an astounding revelation . . . !

MONTGOMERY. It's all true! Every single word of it!

BARRY. It's really hard to believe. You should have told us all this before.

MONTGOMERY. Why?

BARRY. Well, I think it would have made you feel a whole lot better, that's why.

MONTGOMERY. Yeah, I guess you're right.

BARRY. What about broads, Montgomery? You know: chicks?

GEORGIA. *Women*, Barry, *women!*

BARRY. What . . . ?

UTA. *Not* broads, Barry, and *not* chicks, Barry, but *women!*

BARRY. Oh? Well, *women* then. What about women, Montgomery?

NORMA JEAN. You can call us anything you like, Barry! I love men so much! I'm not fussy what men call us!

GEORGIA. Darling: you're *not* fussy over what men call *you!* But don't include *us!* (GEORGIA *gives* UTA *a wink of the eye.*)

NORMA JEAN. Well, I'm just such a complete woman, that's all . . .

UTA. Oh, Christ . . .

NORMA JEAN. I mean I'm so secure about being a woman in relation to all men . . .

GEORGIA. Can you believe her?

NORMA JEAN. That it really just doesn't matter to me what they call me, or all other women for that matter. Of course, I'm not really that interested in all other women for that matter. I'm only interested in all men: that's what really matters.

UTA. I can't believe her at all.

GEORGIA. I guess we just won't pay attention from here on in.

NORMA JEAN. (*Suddenly blurting it out.*) Stop it! Goddammit! You two! Who do you two think you two are?! I'm a human being, too, you know?! There's just so much a person can take! And I'm telling you both right now: I can't take anymore of your bullshit! (NORMA JEAN *grabs her pocketbook.*)

BARRY. Where you going, Norma Jean? (NORMA JEAN *heads towards the door.*)

NORMA JEAN. I'm going back home! Back to my apartment!

BARRY. Aw, c'mon . . .

NORMA JEAN. I'm so fucking fed up!

MONTGOMERY. Don't go, Norma Jean.

NORMA JEAN. I just don't feel wanted here all of a sudden.

GEORGIA. That's not true, Norma Jean. I invited you because I wanted you.

UTA. Forget what we've said, please . . . ?

GEORGIA. Uta's right, darling. (NORMA JEAN *moves back into the living-room again.*)

NORMA JEAN. I feel like I'm going to cry.

GEORGIA. If it'll make you feel better, then by all means: do it.

UTA. It might be the best thing for you.

NORMA JEAN. I'll make another drink first and then see what happens. (NORMA JEAN *goes and makes herself another drink. There is a brief silence. And then* NORMA JEAN *begins to drink her new drink.*)

BARRY. (*Finally, to* MONTGOMERY.) Hey, man! Like I was asking you before: what about broads—I mean *women!* What about you and women in real life, Montgomery?

MONTGOMERY. In real life, well, it's really beginning to be okay now. It was really bad news in the beginning because I was just plain scared stiff when I was with women in real life. But lately, well, it's really getting to be okay. Of course they're very understanding and very gentle and very kind and very careful: all of the women that I know in real life these days.

UTA. I'll bet they all love you . . .

MONTGOMERY. I don't know about that now: but they're all real nice to me. I think it's all because they think I'm a real challenge, and, of course, they're all wrong. I'm not a real challenge at all. I want them more than they could ever know in a million years.

UTA. They're all so lucky, these women you're talking about. They're lucky because they've been given the chance to sleep with you, Montgomery. But they're also lucky because they're not someone like me. They've never been to a hypnotist, I'm sure, and they've never been a strict vegetarian, they've never gone to EST, they've probably never had a shrink, they've never heard of the Daily Word, they've never thought of converting to the Roman Catholic Church, they've probably never been into T.M., and Yoga, and all of that other available *shit!* Sorry, Georgia.

GEORGIA. What are you sorry for?

UTA. For the word: *shit*.

GEORGIA. Oh, well, I didn't even hear it. It must be the booze.

BARRY. Ah, the booze!

UTA. Those women are all so lucky, Montgomery. Lucky to be with you, but even luckier to be just plain downright women and just plain downright human beings and just plain downright beautiful individuals.

GEORGIA. I don't quite know what you're getting at, Uta, but it still sounds convincing: whatever it is.

NORMA JEAN. At this stage of the game, and by this time of the night: I think that I agree. (BARRY *sits down on the floor in the middle of the living-room.*)

BARRY. Do you all realize that most people would be jealous of the five of us? I mean: they should be jealous of the five of us. They *are* jealous of the five of us!

MONTGOMERY. Don't kid yourself, Barry.

BARRY. You don't think so, then, huh?

MONTGOMERY. That's right, man. (MONTGOMERY *goes to the bar in order to make himself another drink.*)

BARRY. Oh, well: maybe it's, at least for me, that I'm kidding myself.

GEORGIA. We're all kidding ourselves, darling.

NORMA JEAN. I just want to be in the movies with my clothes on, that's all. That's not asking too much, is it now? I know I have problems dealing with nymphomania and all that, and I know how much I just simply love fucking and sucking away on the silver jaded screen and all that . . . I really do. I think you're the only other one, just like me, aren't you, Barry? Who really and truly: deep down inside: digs it as much as I do. On-screen or off-screen: *I just love it!* But only with *men:* do I love it! And that's another problem I'm facing right now: they want me to do my first scene making love with another woman! Can you believe it?! Me?! Never! In a million years! I'm really afraid they'll fire me if I don't. I'll be black-balled if I don't. They feel it'll be big box-office: me making my sexual debut for the first time on the silver jaded screen with some other woman. Well, I can't stand it! It makes me sick even to think about it!

BARRY. Oh, wow! (BARRY *begins to laugh.*)

NORMA JEAN. What's so funny, Barry? (BARRY *is really laughing now.*)

BARRY. It might make you sick to think about it, baby, but it's making me get so turned-on just thinking about it! I feel like jacking-off—sorry, Georgia!—*masturbating* for the first time in real life with an audience sitting around me: that's how turned-on I am about the whole idea, Norma Jean! (GEORGIA *goes to the sofa and lies down upon it; she is laughing with* BARRY.)

NORMA JEAN. Listen, I don't care what you're all thinking . . .

MONTGOMERY. (*Chuckling.*) I'm gonna split a gut. (MONTGOMERY *sits down on the window sill ledge.*)

NORMA JEAN. But I can make it anywhere . . .

UTA. (*Laughing with the rest of them now.*) I think you should be on television, Norma Jean, on Saturday nights, prime-time! (UTA *sits on a high pile of pillows.*)

NORMA JEAN. I can make it anytime, and all of the time, anywhere and everywhere! But I'm tired of it now! I'm out of control because of it, and it's driving me crazy because of it! I would do anything at this stage of the game to solve my pressing problem of nymphomania, and all of the pressing things related to it: I really want to have control again: so badly! (*They are all still laughing together;* NORMA JEAN *lets out a piercing scream, and runs away from them all; they all stop laughing instantly together.*) No, no, no! I really mean it! And I don't know if I ever told any of you this before: but I've got this adorable little boy who's living in California right now, and do you know what, Georgia, everybody? Today is *his* birthday too! He's ten years old today . . . my adorable little boy out in California. I had him when I was just sweet sixteen. I was so young. I didn't know what I was doing. I was so out of control then, just the way I'm so out of control now. I got married so fast and then just as fast: I lost him. His father took him away from me. I was caught "fooling around" behind the bowling alley. It was awful. It's all just, well, it's just driving me up the walls these days! I would do anything to solve my problems. If I became a real actress, a real legitimate star who could be on the stage and win a Tony and be on the screen and win an Oscar, if I could do that, well, I just know that all my problems would be solved . . . ! (*There is an uneasy silence.*) Georgia . . . ?

GEORGIA. Yes, darling.

NORMA JEAN. Would you do me a favor?

GEORGIA. Of course.

NORMA JEAN. I would like to call him. My little boy. Just because it's his birthday too.

GEORGIA. Of course you can call him.

NORMA JEAN. Thank you so much. Just as soon as I get it together: that's when I'll do it. I need some more time. But that's okay: it's three hour's difference in California, so that's really okay. Everything's going to be okay. (*A pause.*) Of course everything's going to be okay! Remember my secret, everybody?! My secret little surprise?! Well, it's not really that little: it's really very big: my surprise: Georgia's birthday present, and, in the end: a birthday present for all of us.

GEORGIA. (*Getting up.*) Do you know what I think? I think that I should open up my presents from Barry and Uta so that we can hear what my present from Norma Jean is. We already know what your present is, don't we, Montgomery? And it's beautiful and I'll never let it die, either.

MONTGOMERY. That's the way I like to hear you talk.

UTA. My present is really rather silly. I made it myself.

NORMA JEAN. Oh, I love presents like that!

BARRY. Yeah? Well, I bought mine. (GEORGIA *begins to unwrap the present from* UTA.)

GEORGIA. Oh, my God: it's lovely. It's a scarf for my head. It's beautiful, Uta. I love the design and everything else about it. And the fact that you made it: I'm really impressed by that. Thank you, darling. (GEORGIA *passes the beautiful-looking scarf around to all of them.*)

BARRY. Here's mine, Georgia. (BARRY *hands his gift to* GEORGIA *again. She begins to open it.*)

GEORGIA. Oh, my God: it's a ring! A bright red-rock ring encased in gleaming gold! Thank you, Barry darling.

BARRY. Don't mention it.

BARRY. It's nice, don't you think?

NORMA JEAN. It's beautiful.

UTA. It really is.

MONTGOMERY. It matches the blood-red buds of the birthday plant. (GEORGIA *exits.*)

BARRY. Hey, Georgia! Where you goin'?!

GEORGIA. (*Offstage.*) I'm bringing in my birthday cake!

BARRY. (*After a pause.*) I'll . . . I'll go in and help her . . . (BARRY *exits.*)

MONTGOMERY. I'm really beginning to feel high. I'm beginning to feel right at home here. I'm beginning to love it here. I guess it's like a womb or something, if you know what I mean . . . ?

UTA. I know what you mean.

NORMA JEAN. (*Starting to drift away.*) Georgia's birthday party! I love it! And just wait until I tell you what I've been keeping a secret all night.

MONTGOMERY. Yeah, that's right.

UTA. Secrets, secrets, secrets! (UTA *gives* MONTGOMERY *a shy stare; he returns it.*)

MONTGOMERY. (*To* UTA.) It was beautiful . . .

UTA. What was . . . ? (NORMA JEAN *lies down on the sofa and closes her eyes.*)

MONTGOMERY. That scarf you made for Georgia.

UTA. It was nothing, really . . .

MONTGOMERY. I love scarves . . .

UTA. I'd love to make you one . . .

MONTGOMERY. Honest . . . ?

UTA. Really . . .

MONTGOMERY. That's awfully nice of you . . .

UTA. It's nothing, really . . .

MONTGOMERY. When you find the time, okay . . . ?

UTA. Okay . . . (*It looks as though* NORMA JEAN *might be sleeping by this time on the sofa.*)

MONTGOMERY. I really think . . .

UTA. Yes . . . ?

MONTGOMERY. I really feel . . .

UTA. Yes . . . ?

MONTGOMERY. Aw, forget it, I guess . . .

UTA. No, please . . .

MONTGOMERY. Well, I really think, and I really feel . . .

UTA. Please say it . . .

MONTGOMERY. Aw, I really better forget it.

UTA. No, don't: please . . . ?

MONTGOMERY. I'm just such a lousy sayer of things. I'm such a lousy talker. I really don't speak out the way I would like to speak out. Do you know what I mean?

UTA. Yes, I do.

MONTGOMERY. Do you find it hard to talk to people you really want to talk to?

UTA. It's awful, I know.

MONTGOMERY. Do you know something?

UTA. What's that?

MONTGOMERY. I can't believe that I'm finding it so easy to carry on a conversation with you.

UTA. It's really very good for me to hear someone say something like that to me . . . especially someone like you. Thank you.

(BARRY *enters, alone. He carries a small birthday cake with eight burning pink candles; he begins to sing "Happy Birthday" while the sparkler-flare in the middle of the cake makes hissing, blinking light.*)

BARRY. (*Singing.*) Happy Birthday to you . . . (GEORGIA *enters now.* MONTGOMERY *and* UTA *turn to face them and then they both join in singing with* BARRY.)

BARRY, MONTGOMERY, UTA. (*Singing.*) Happy Birthday to you, Happy Birthday to you, Happy Birthday, dear Georgia, Happy Birthday to you! (BARRY, MONTGOMERY, *and* UTA *clap their hands happily for* GEORGIA.)

GEORGIA. Oh, thank you! Thank you all! I really appreciate it all so much! (GEORGIA *turns to face the sleeping* NORMA JEAN.)

GEORGIA. My God! Norma Jean's asleep! What an extra-special surprise birthday present! (NORMA JEAN *begins to stir on the sofa.*)

NORMA JEAN. I heard that!

GEORGIA. Oh, dear! (GEORGIA *immediately blows out the eight candles on her birthday cake.*)

NORMA JEAN. Oh, did I hear that! (GEORGIA *looks up at everyone as they applaud her for blowing all of the candles out at once.*)

BARRY. Right on, baby!

MONTGOMERY. Outa sight, miss!

UTA. Congratulations! (GEORGIA *begins to take the candles from out of the birthday cake.*)

NORMA JEAN. All right, you four super-duper stars! What have I been missing? Whose birthday party is this anyway? Hell, I really don't care whose birthday party it is because you all give the impression of having a wonderful time, and so, I suppose that I'm supposed to be having a wonderful time too. (NORMA JEAN *sits up in the sofa.*) And now it's the exact right time for me to give you the birthday present I was telling you about, Georgia.

GEORGIA. It better be good.

NORMA JEAN. Oh, it's good all right. It's good for all of us, like I told you all before. I met a man yesterday afternoon, and this man turned out to be very rich and somewhat young and strangely, wildly handsome. The minute his eyes fell upon me I knew that I had his complete and unselfish attention. But the most important thing of all, everybody, is that he's a playwright.

GEORGIA. A playwright?

NORMA JEAN. Right! A playwright!

BARRY. Is he a good playwright?

MONTGOMERY. That's just what I was going to ask.

UTA. Is he famous?

NORMA JEAN. Will you all please let me finish?!

GEORGIA. Yes, will you please let her finish, all of you. After all, all of you: this *is* my birthday present from her.

NORMA JEAN. Georgia's right. And so, this very rich, somewhat young, and strangely, wildly handsome playwright recognized me immediately. He's seen all my films. He's seen almost all your films too. He loves me. He also loves the four of you. Do you know what he wants to do? He wants to write a play just for the five of us. He told me that all of the roles will be equal and we'll all be onstage just about all of the time. Isn't that wonderful?!

NORMA JEAN. And there's no problem with a theater, either. He's also going to produce it because of all his money. I hope you don't mind, Georgia, but do you know what I did?

NORMA JEAN. I gave him your address and your telephone number. But I also invited him to come by here tonight. He said he would be here by midnight.

BARRY. It's almost midnight now. (*He looks at his wristwatch.*)

UTA. Well, we really have something to look forward to.

MONTGOMERY. Was he really on the level?

NORMA JEAN. Oh, without a doubt. His name is Christopher Rock, and I also let him ball me. We balled for eight hours at his beautiful triplex apartment on Park Avenue. Listen: if he writes plays the way he balls, well, forget it! We're in business, all of us! And so, Happy Birthday once again, Georgia sweetheart.

GEORGIA. Well, thank you.

NORMA JEAN. Well, you don't sound very happy about it.

BARRY. I don't know about her, but I'm getting real positive vibes.

MONTGOMERY. So am I.

UTA. Me too. (NORMA JEAN *goes to make herself another drink.* GEORGIA *begins to cut the birthday cake.*)

GEORGIA. Well, it's certainly time for some birthday cake now: for extra-celebrating now.

BARRY. Never mind about the birthday cake . . .

MONTGOMERY. Yeah, Georgia . . .

UTA. What about *your* secret?

NORMA JEAN. Oh, yes, that's right, Georgia sweetheart, let's hear it. (GEORGIA *begins to pass the pieces of birthday cake around to all of them.*)

GEORGIA. All right then. Guess what? I'm pregnant. Can you believe it?! I'm going to have a baby! After all of these years and after all of the endless countless painful mishaps and mistakes and miscarriages: I am finally pregnant again. And this time, no matter what: I'm going to do everything imaginable to have it. It can be a boy it can be a girl it can be twin boys or twin girls or a twin boy and a twin girl, it can be anything it wants to be: as long as I can go ahead and have it.

BARRY. This is really hard to believe, Georgia.

MONTGOMERY. When did it happen?

NORMA JEAN. Most important of all: who is the father? And are you going to marry him? (*There is a long pause; they all look at one another except* GEORGIA: *she seems rather extra-radiant now.*)

GEORGIA. I think we need some music at this point. (GEORGIA *puts on a record; it is rather rocky-and-raunchy-sounding.*)

MONTGOMERY. It's really been a terrific birthday party so far. And we have so much more to look forward to tonight. The coming of the playwright, for instance. And the coming of Georgia's baby, later on, for instance. I'm really beginning to feel high and happy.

UTA. The coming of the playwright could be such a blessing for all of us. He could be our saviour, or something like that. I can hardly wait for him to show up. (BARRY *remains quiet. He is both half-sad-looking and half-puzzled-looking.*)

GEORGIA. Aw, Barry darling!

BARRY. What . . . ?

GEORGIA. Cat's got your tongue?

BARRY. I think so. (GEORGIA *gives* BARRY *a forkfull of birthday cake.*)

GEORGIA. (*Beginning to sing with the music.*) Thirty-five pink candles we will take, Put them on a birthday cake, All for Georgia, Holy sakes, Georgia's thirty-five years . . . old! *Young!* (MONTGOMERY *claps his hands and begins to move his body in relation to the sensuous raunchy-rock music.* GEORGIA *begins to dance too.*)

GEORGIA and MONTGOMERY. (*Singing and dancing.*) Thirty-five pink candles we will take, Put them on a birthday cake, All for Georgia, Holy sakes, Georgia's thirty-five years . . . old! *Young!* (UTA *and* NORMA JEAN *begin to dance also now.*)

UTA and NORMA JEAN. (*Singing and dancing.*) Thirty-five pink candles we will take, Put them on a birthday cake, All for Georgia, Holy sakes, Georgia's thirty-five years . . . old! *Young!*

GEORGIA. C'mon darling Barry. (GEORGIA *takes* BARRY *by the hand as they all dance and sing together now: it is very sexual and sensuous without any of them really knowing it.*)

ALL. (*Singing and dancing.*) Thirty-five pink candles we will take, Put them on a birthday cake, All for Georgia, Holy sakes, Georgia's thirty-five years . . . old! *Young!*

(*The music comes way up.* BARRY *breaks away from them.*

And then GEORGIA *breaks away from them too.* MONT-GOMERY, UTA, *and* NORMA JEAN *continue to dance wildly, singing a repeat of the song.* GEORGIA *stands silently in the center of the room, staring at the back of* BARRY, *who is looking off into space somewhere. And then, slowly, he turns to face* GEORGIA: *both of them: silent, serious, pensive. The lights come way up, bright and beaming. And then slowly, there is a fading dim-out.*)

CURTAIN

ACT TWO

When the lights come up we hear music coming from the radio. The music is very soft and very sweet and very gentle. It reminds us almost of some child's lullaby. All five of them are sleeping: and they are all sleeping alone: GEORGIA *is asleep on the floor in an upright position, her back and head resting against the sofa;* NORMA JEAN *is sprawled out on her back on the sofa itself;* UTA *is sleeping opposite them in the same position as* GEORGIA'S *with her back and head resting against the bar;* MONTGOMERY *is sprawled out on his back on the window sill ledge;* BARRY *is stretched out on his back on the floor directly in the middle of the living-room. Finally, it is* MONTGOMERY *who wakes up first. He looks all about the living-room. His eyes eventually end up on the figure of* UTA. *Slowly, quietly,* MONTGOMERY *leaves the window sill ledge and crawls along the floor until he reaches* UTA. *He places his head in her lap and then goes back to sleep. Eventually,* GEORGIA *wakes up. She also gives the living-room a complete going-over until her eyes finally remain on the sleeping body of* BARRY. *Then, very slowly, carefully,* GEORGIA *crawls across the floor to* BARRY *and lies down next to him with her arm around his waist; she also goes back to sleep. Presently,* NORMA JEAN *begins to stir in her sleep and then she begins to talk in her sleep.*

NORMA JEAN. (*In her sleep.*) Oh, there, that's right, *there!* Oh, oh, oh! You're hurting me but I love it! You're going to kill me but I love it! Oh, you're not too big and you're not too small. You're just right in there. You're perfect in there. Oh, you have such a nice . . . It's perfectly nice, it really is! Perfectly nice is a whole lot better than too big. Too big is a bore. You can't do things with it when it's too big. But oh, oh, oh! When it's perfectly nice the way yours is perfectly nice, well, it's freer, it moves better, it's just like an acrobat, or it's just like having an underweight champion jockey on his horse in there! Oh, oh, oh! Don't come yet! Oh! Oh! Oh! OOOOOOO . . . Christopher *Rock!* I just love your perfectly nice playwright's *cock!* OH! OH! OH! Ahhhhhhh! Ahhhhhhh . . . (NORMA JEAN *wakes up.*) Where am I? Oh? Now I know where I am. I'm here. Exactly where I was the last time. Well, will you just take a look at all of them now? Two pairs of lovebirds. Actually, it's quite lovely. I love it. I wish I wouldn't feel so jealous, though. Jealousy is such a waste of time. And I hate to waste my time, and so, well, I've just got to control myself: I've got to control my jealousy. What time is it anyway? (*She looks at her wristwatch.*) Oh, my God! It's two-thirty in the morning. Where is he? My playwright who was supposed to come? Christopher Rock! He didn't even call. (*She pauses; she is rather sad now.*) He could have at least called . . . (NORMA JEAN *tiptoes to the bar. She makes herself a fresh new drink.*) They all look so, well, so perfectly nice. If only I could control my jealousy. But really now: they should be jealous of *me!* I'm the one who gave them the contact with the playwright, whenever he comes. I'm the one who enjoys sex more than they could ever enjoy it. I'm the one who could become a serious actress way before they ever could. I'm the one who has the real star quality which could make me known throughout the whole wide world. (*She looks at the telephone.*) Why didn't he call . . . ? (*She takes a large swig of her drink.*) I'm getting mad now. All right, everybody: get up, get up, get up! I'm jealous! And so you have to GET UP! ALL FOUR OF YOU! (NORMA JEAN *goes to* MONTGOMERY *and* UTA; *she gives them both pokes.*)

MONTGOMERY. (*Waking up.*) What's going on . . . ?

NORMA JEAN. Time to get up.

UTA. (*Waking up.*) Why . . . ?

NORMA JEAN. Because this is a party, that's why. (NORMA JEAN *goes and gives pokes to* GEORGIA *and* BARRY.) Time to get up.

BARRY. (*Waking up.*) What are you talking about . . . ?

NORMA JEAN. C'mon, get up.

GEORGIA. (*Waking up.*) What time is it?

NORMA JEAN. It's two-thirty in the morning.

MONTGOMERY. Where's the playwright who was supposed to come?

UTA. Did he come while we were all sleeping?

NORMA JEAN. I'm sorry . . .

BARRY. He never came, did he?

NORMA JEAN. I said I was sorry . . .

GEORGIA. Did he call at least?

NORMA JEAN. No . . .

GEORGIA. Well, *some* playwright, that's all I can say.

NORMA JEAN. I think I'm going crazy.

GEORGIA. Relax, darling.

NORMA JEAN. How can I relax?! I've been stood up! I've never been stood up before! You've all been stood up too! I'm so embarrassed.

BARRY. Forget it, baby.

MONTGOMERY. Barry's right . . .

UTA. And so is Georgia.

NORMA JEAN. It's easy for her to say.

MONTGOMERY. Why do you say that?

NORMA JEAN. Well, you've all got one another. Who have I got?

GEORGIA. You've got all of us . . .

MONTGOMERY. That's who you've got.

UTA. The hell with your playwright-friend. We don't need him, after all, do we, everybody?

GEORGIA. Agreed.

BARRY. He's a prick! (GEORGIA *puts her hand over* BARRY's *mouth.*)

MONTGOMERY. He's an asshole! He must be a fag too. You said he saw all of us in our flicks, which means he saw me in my fag flicks. He's a fag, so forget about him. You know how much I hate fags. I hate all faggots! They should have their cocks cut off and their assholes welded shut with solid lead.

UTA. He sounds like a dirty old man to me. But I guess he really isn't a dirty old man, after all. He's a dirty rich young playwright who doesn't keep his word. That's even worse than being a dirty old man. I hate him too.

BARRY. Life is but a dream . . . who said that, by the way?

MONTGOMERY. My favorite playwright, by the way. Luigi Pirandello. Now that's a playwright for you. Not like this creep you been telling us about, Norma Jean. (NORMA JEAN *continues to drink her drink.*)

NORMA JEAN. Well, let me tell you something.

BARRY. Life is but a dream! And so, Norma Jean: you dreamt about your playwright who was supposed to come! Forget it! Leave it at that!

GEORGIA. Hey, Barry darling, relax.

BARRY. I'm up to here! Dreams! Playwrights! Babies! I'm going to the shithouse . . . ! (BARRY *exits.*)

MONTGOMERY. (*Calling after him.*) I'm next!

UTA. (*To* MONTGOMERY.) And I'm after you.

MONTGOMERY. No you're not. Ladies before gentlemen.

UTA. No way. I don't believe in that.

MONTGOMERY. Okay for you . . .

UTA. But that doesn't mean that I don't like you . . .

GEORGIA. Did you know that that is the title of my next flick?

MONTGOMERY. What is?

GEORGIA. Life is but a dream! And it will be history-making, because the movie will run for almost two hours and I'll be completely nude the entire time! No one has ever appeared totally naked on the screen for such a long period of time. What a bore! It will also be my last flick before my baby. It's really quite wonderful, in a way, because the part calls for a woman who is in early pregnancy. So you see . . . all of you . . . and Barry too . . . far off somewhere in the bathroom: everything works out just simply perfect in the end. And that's what I want to tell you, Norma Jean: that everything just simply works out perfectly in the end. But of course I believe in all that simply because I also don't believe that "life is but a dream." Quite the opposite: *it's real!*

NORMA JEAN. I don't agree with you.

GEORGIA. You don't have to, but I think you should.

NORMA JEAN. Well, I don't think I should.

GEORGIA. You, more than anybody else here, you should really agree with me.

NORMA JEAN. What does that mean?

GEORGIA. It means that *you* should really listen to me.

NORMA JEAN. Why should I listen to something I disagree with?

GEORGIA. But you haven't let me finish.

NORMA JEAN. Because I know what you're going to say.

GEORGIA. I don't think you do.

NORMA JEAN. You're going to repeat yourself. You're going to tell me that "life is not a dream." And then you're going to tell me that life is real. And then I'm going to repeat myself again too: by telling you that I disagree with you.

GEORGIA. Listen, darling: I'm with you, I'm on your side. So why are you fighting me?

NORMA JEAN. Who says I'm fighting you?

GEORGIA. It doesn't have to be said: it's in the tone of your voice.

NORMA JEAN. What tone in my voice?

GEORGIA. There, right now: that defensive tone: you just did it.

NORMA JEAN. Oh, I just want to be left alone, that's all.

GEORGIA. I just think that I can help you, that's all.

NORMA JEAN. Well, forget it! The only way you can help me right now is by not thinking that you can help me right now: that's the only way!

GEORGIA. All right then: but don't get so excited.

NORMA JEAN. Who's getting excited?!

GEORGIA. You are. Just listen to you.

NORMA JEAN. Better I listen to myself at this point, rather than have to listen to you at this point.

GEORGIA. All right then: have it your way. (NORMA JEAN *pours herself another drink.*)

NORMA JEAN. I'm going to have my way by meditating.

GEORGIA. Meditating?

NORMA JEAN. That's what I said. (NORMA JEAN *goes to the sofa.*)

GEORGIA. Well, you just do whatever makes you feel good. (NORMA JEAN *sprawls out on the sofa with her drink.*)

NORMA JEAN. I'm going to try. (NORMA JEAN *nods her head negatively: like a spoiled little child now.*)

MONTGOMERY. (*After a pause.*) I really was looking forward to the playwright coming. I've got to admit that.

UTA. We all were. We'd be lying if we said otherwise. (*A pause.*) I thought to myself earlier: this is it! This is the big break for me! For all of us! There were butterflies in my stomach and my head started to ache even. But it was a rather pleasant sort of ache simply because I thought to myself: well, this is finally it! We'll show the world what true artists we really are, after all. Maybe life is a dream. Maybe it was a dream. Not just Norma Jean's dream. But Montgomerys' dream, and Georgia's dream, and Barry's dream, and my dream.

MONTGOMERY. My life in art! A fucking joke!

UTA. I'm getting sad all of a sudden.

GEORGIA. Don't!

UTA. It's all so hard. It really is. (NORMA JEAN *is half-falling-asleep again.*)

NORMA JEAN. (*Mumbling.*) You're fucking-A right it is
. . . !
GEORGIA. Listen to her.
MONTGOMERY. She's falling asleep again.
NORMA JEAN. I'm not falling asleep again! I'm meditating!
UTA. Let her be then.
GEORGIA. We'll even talk quiet for her, won't we?
MONTGOMERY. Just so long as she doesn't wake up.
NORMA JEAN. How can I wake up when I'm not sleeping?!
UTA. She's so lucky she can doze off the way she does
. . .
NORMA JEAN. I said I'm meditating, goddammitt!
UTA. I wish I could do it. I'm still spending a fortune on sleeping pills and other things.
GEORGIA. That's not too good, Uta.
UTA. Don't you think I know that?
GEORGIA. It's good I'm going to have this baby. It will keep me off all of the pills and all of the dope and all of the booze. I want this kid real bad, and you better believe it! Having this baby is not a dream. It's real. The only thing that's really a dream is what we're all doing, all five of us: it's a real bad dream. It's a real nightmare! But, of course, what I'm really saying is that what we're all doing is so real, so downright real, so downright *rotten* real, that no matter what: it could ruin all of us in the end! It's about time the rest of you started thinking this way. I've got a few years on all of you and so I only think it's right that you all listen to me. It's what I was really going to say to Norma Jean before, but she wouldn't let me. I think that you should quit the whole sick sordid scene, I really do. What's going to happen when you all get older? How are you going to deal with the wrinkles on your skin, and the bumps and lumps all over your bodies? How are you going to accept the double chins and the sagging breasts and the flabby bellies? We're all supposed to grow old gracefully and beautifully, so get

out of it now, so that you have the chance to grow gracefully and beautifully old. About a year ago I was sitting in a beauty parlor having my hair done. None of the women knew who I was. And so I just sat there and listened to their conversation. One of the women was talking about the first porno movie she had ever seen. She was shocked and sick by it all. She told some of the other women about a woman who was about the same age as all of them—forty-five or fifty—and how this woman did things on the screen by herself, such shocking things, that this woman who was telling the story was just too embarrassed to even hint at what the woman on the screen was doing to herself. One of the other women in the beauty parlor then made the remark: "I wonder what happens to a woman like that in *real* life. I mean I wonder how a woman like that can make it through the day in her everyday *real* life. I wonder what happens to her when she's at home alone and not before the cameras." And then one of the other women in the beauty parlor said: "Well, I just wonder what happens to people like that period. I mean, eventually, when they get older, how do they end up?" Well, there was a short pause between all of the women in the beauty parlor, and then, finally, one of them said: "Well, I'm sure that there are only two ways: they either go insane or they kill themselves." Well, kids, let me tell you something: three days after that little discussion in the beauty parlor, Miss Paulette Love, that woman who did such shocking things by herself on the screen, things that were sickening and too embarrassing to even hint at, well, Miss Paulette Love committed suicide, she killed herself by injecting an old United States army rifle all the way up her vagina, and then, after shoving it in-and-out: she pulled the trigger. And then, of course, there's the story of the young Mr. Wayne Cassidy-Newman—I know you've heard of him—who used to call himself Elvis Jagger, remember? Well, Mr. Wayne Cassidy-Newman is hidden somewhere in some hospital somewhere, and just last week a lobotomy . . . there was nothing else that they could do. And that's it, kiddies . . . !

MONTGOMERY. What a crock! What a crock of shit! I don't believe any of it! Any of it! Any of it! (BARRY *lets out a wild scream from the bathroom.*)

GEORGIA. Oh, my God!

MONTGOMERY. (*Calling.*) What's the matter?! (BARRY *continues to scream. They are all just about ready to head towards the bathroom when* BARRY *appears: holding his belt and clutching at his pants at the waist.*)

BARRY. (*Hysterical.*) I've got a boil on my ass! I've got this huge boil on my ass right smack in the middle of my left cheek! Oh, I can't stand it! Oh, God, why did this have to happen to me now?! I've got ten closeups of my ass in solid action scheduled for Thursday! They'll never be able to do it now! I hate it! I hate it when something goes physically wrong with me! I've been so careful too! I don't understand it. It's awful! I've got the most beautiful set of masculine buns on the screen today!

MONTGOMERY. No, I have.

BARRY. What did you say?!

MONTGOMERY. I said I've got to go to the bathroom.

BARRY. That isn't what you said, man!

MONTGOMERY. I did too.

BARRY. No, you didn't!

GEORGIA. Yes, he did.

UTA. Georgia's right, Barry. (GEORGIA *exits suddenly into her bedroom.*)

BARRY. Maybe it's because I'm so nervous all of a sudden. It was awful in the bathroom just now. First I had to pee, and I really peed a whole lot, like it was never going to stop, like I thought all of the water was coming out of my system and I would die from it; and then I had to do number two, too, and it really hurt when it all came out, tons of it, like I was filled up with nothing but garbage and like I didn't have a heart or a liver or glands or anything else like that: only tons of shit; and then, to make things worse, I had to throw-up too! I threw-up for all five of us, let me tell you! I threw-up for the whole goddam country the way it all came gushing out of my poor delicate sensitive humanly human system! (GEORGIA *enters. She is wearing a white-gold satin bathrobe.*)

GEORGIA. Yeah, well: you poor baby.

BARRY. (*Weakly.*) Thanks, Georgia.

UTA. I'll bet you feel a whole lot better now, don't you, Barry?

BARRY. (*Like a little kid.*) I don't know . . . (GEORGIA *goes to* BARRY *and gives him a light kiss on the lips.*)

GEORGIA. What would you like now, darling?

BARRY. Another drink, that's what I would like now.

GEORGIA. Anything you say. (GEORGIA *goes and makes* BARRY *another drink.*)

BARRY. (*Looking at* NORMA JEAN.) How the hell does she do it?

UTA. We'd all like to know.

GEORGIA. She has no guilt.

UTA. I'll bet that's it.

GEORGIA. That's exactly what it is. (GEORGIA *hands* BARRY *a fresh new drink.*)

UTA. Life is but a nightmare! Right, Barry?

BARRY. You better believe it, Uta!

UTA. But not really. I was just being funny, Barry.

BARRY. Well, I'm sorry: but I just don't feel like laughing now.

GEORGIA. Life is but a beautiful dream, and that's all there is to it, right, darling Barry?! Who could ask for anything more? I think it's a lovely description of life: simply: a beautiful dream. Like I said before: who could ask for anything more?

BARRY. While I was in the bathroom . . . ?

GEORGIA. Yes . . . ?

BARRY. Did that playwright happen to call?

GEORGIA. No.

BARRY. Rat fink, mother . . . !

GEORGIA. Be sweet and cool, darling. (MONTGOMERY *moans in the background.*)

GEORGIA. Who's moaning now, for Christ's sake?! Montgomery?!

MONTGOMERY. I just want to act, that's all. I want the stage, that's all. I wanted the playwright to show up, that's all. I just got a headache, that's all.

GEORGIA. I feel like a very professional nurse: a combination of Florence Nightingale and Clara Barton and Sister Carrie.

BARRY. I never heard of any of them.

MONTGOMERY. I did.

BARRY. Well, big deal, man! Just because you read a lot!

MONTGOMERY. So what's wrong with that, man?!

BARRY. What are you gettin' pissed about?!

MONTGOMERY. I'm not getting pissed! You're the one who's getting pissed! (*The telephone rings.*)

GEORGIA. Oh, my God! It's the playwright!

BARRY. Answer it!

GEORGIA. I wouldn't know what to say! (*The telephone rings again.*)

UTA. Answer it, Georgia, please!

GEORGIA. I'm a nervous wreck! (*The telephone rings again.*)

MONTGOMERY. Aw, c'mon, Georgia, please?!

BARRY. Do you want me to answer it?!

GEORGIA. Norma Jean, Norma Jean, Norma Jean?! (*The telephone rings again. They all sit there, or stand there, like statues.* NORMA JEAN *begins to stir on the sofa.*) Norma Jean?! IT'S THE PLAYWRIGHT, NORMA JEAN! (NORMA JEAN *jumps up off the sofa.*)

NORMA JEAN. Oh, my God! You're right! (NORMA JEAN *runs to the telephone, but by the time she gets there it stops ringing. She picks up the receiver. All five of them look as though the world has caved in on them.* NORMA JEAN *desperately.*) Hello?! Hello?! Hello?! HELLO?! (*There is dead silence.* NORMA JEAN *hangs up the telephone.*)

GEORGIA. (*Finally.*) Maybe . . . he'll try again. (*All five of them wait; nothing happens. Finally.*) It's my fault. I'm so sorry, I really am. Please forgive me: all of you. (*Dead silence. Finally.*) Maybe he's calling from a public telephone, maybe he ran out of change, maybe . . . (*Dead silence. Finally.*) Well, say something! Any of you! Will you please say something?! I can't stand it! (*Dead silence. One-by-one they all make themselves brand-new fresh drinks. Then, one-by-one, they bring their drinks with them and they all sit down on the floor around the telephone. They wait. Finally.*) Maybe he's got more change by this time. (*Suddenly, the telephone rings again.* NORMA JEAN *picks it up immediately. They all look at each other with great relief.*)

NORMA JEAN. (*Into the telephone.*) Hello?! Oh, it's *you!* How nice of *you* to call like this! Yes, yes: we're all here. Yes, we've been waiting all night. Oh, you did? We must've been asleep. Oh, it's all right. No, no, no. You don't have to apologize. We all understand. (*A long pause as* NORMA JEAN *listens.*) Yes. All right then. (*Another pause as she continues to listen.*) I understand. No, it's all right. I said I understand, so it's really okay. I'd love to, Mr. Rock. Christopher. In a half-hour. Of course. I'll see you then. Good-bye. And thanks so much for calling, Christopher. (NORMA JEAN *hangs up.*)

GEORGIA. What happened?!

BARRY. Is he coming?!

MONTGOMERY. What did he say to you?!

UTA. Is everything going to work out okay for all of us?! (NORMA JEAN *begins to pick up her belongings.*)

NORMA JEAN. I don't know what to say but I'd better say it anyway. I'm really sorry, but what can I tell you all? He's really not interested in the four of you, after all. He said he was drunk when he told me what he told me. He didn't mean a word of it.

GEORGIA. Didn't mean . . . a word of it . . . ?

NORMA JEAN. He said he never wrote a play in his life.

BARRY. I don't believe it . . .

NORMA JEAN. He says he does things like that a lot when he gets too drunk.

MONTGOMERY. He does things like that . . . a lot . . . ?

NORMA JEAN. He says to tell all of you that he's sorry.

UTA. He's sorry . . . ?

(*Dead silence.* NORMA JEAN *is just about ready to leave. She looks at them all. She feels just as bad as they do in her own individual way.*)

NORMA JEAN. He wants me to come over to his place in a half-hour. I wouldn't mind living there. Maybe he'll ask me to move in with him. I don't know. He could really help me. He has millions of dollars and thousands of the right connections. Maybe this is the end of my porno days and the beginning of my acting career. I don't know. Maybe he's not a playwright after all, but he's just simply wonderful in bed. I don't know . . .

GEORGIA. It's three o'clock right now. What time would that make it in California now?

BARRY. Three hour's difference.

NORMA JEAN. That's right . . .

MONTGOMERY. It's twelve o'clock in California right now.

NORMA JEAN. That's right . . .

UTA. Weren't you going to call your little boy and wish him a happy birthday?

NORMA JEAN. That's right . . .

GEORGIA. I told you that you could use my phone. It's on the house.

BARRY. Ten years old, right?
NORMA JEAN. Right . . .
MONTGOMERY. What's his name?
NORMA JEAN. I forgot . . .
GEORGIA. You sure you don't want to call him, Norma Jean?
NORMA JEAN. Positive! He might not even be home. Or might not even be allowed to come to the phone. Or he might not even want to come to the phone. Listen, I'm a goddamn cliche. Every other hooker in the whole wide world has that little boy or that little girl back in Kansas somewhere. It's a standard story. It's corny . . . and boring. (*There is a short pause now.*) He likes to be urinated upon.
GEORGIA. What . . . ?!
NORMA JEAN. (*Laughing strangely.*) No, not my little boy! My friend. Mr. Rock. Who never wrote a play in his life. He likes that a lot. What can I say? I've done worse things than that on the silver jaded porno screens, haven't I? (*Dead Silence.*) Georgia? Barry? Montgomery? Uta? I loved being here tonight . . . I love, well, I love all of you so much more than you could ever possibly imagine. I love . . .
GEORGIA. (*Finishing her drink.*) You know what?!
NORMA JEAN. You talking to me, Georgia?
GEORGIA. That's exactly who I'm talking to! And do you know what? Well, I'll tell you what! Suddenly, I'm just sick and tired of listening to you use the word love the way you've been using it all night tonight. I've had it up to my weary neck! I am fed up—I AM EXHAUSTED! I am bored! Bored with the way you use the word love! Love—LOVE! LOVE! What the hell do you know about love, Norma Jean? (*Pause.*) You don't know a good goddamn thing about love . . . (*Silence.*) And you wanna know something else? All of you? Well, you're all the same. Talking about boils on your ass—playwrights. What the

hell is another play? Nothing! I don't think any of you know about love, after all. It's all inside, kiddies! Not on the outside, kiddies. I'm in the worst state of fatigue imaginable because I'm so tired of hearing about what you all see in the mirror and what you all see on the screen and what you all spill from your mouths . . . instead of from your hearts and your souls and your goddamn guts! (*Silence*.)

NORMA JEAN. Now wait a minute . . .

GEORGIA. Don't tell me to wait a minute, darling! This is my roof you're under!

NORMA JEAN. What did Uta say earlier about your roof?

GEORGIA. You've really made a sham of things, Norma Jean. You really have.

NORMA JEAN. I was out of control.

GEORGIA. Bullshit!

NORMA JEAN. Listen you . . .

GEORGIA. No, you listen for a change. I am sick and tired of hearing you say you're out of control. You better find a new excuse.

NORMA JEAN. It's not an excuse.

GEORGIA. Drinking all my liquor the way you've been drinking it. I should have forced you to pay for every drop you've had tonight. I'm glad your husband took your little boy away from you, Norma Jean. I really am!

UTA. That's if the little boy exists in the first place!

NORMA JEAN. What?

UTA. You heard me!

NORMA JEAN. You two ladies are turning into just what you really are, after all. A couple of tacky porno stars who couldn't act their ways out of a paper bag!

UTA. The only way you act, honey, is with that greyhound bus terminal you got between your legs.

BARRY. Hey, Uta . . . come on . . .

UTA. Oh, come on, Barry—leave me alone! That's all you got, Norma Jean. Buses going in and buses going out! Tacky old buses filled with tacky old bus passengers.

NORMA JEAN. And what about you. Goddam airline terminal down there! You could easily fit a 747 in there. And there'd still be room in there for an extra bus, and an extra taxicab, and an extra helicopter, and an extra . . .

GEORGIA. Get out of here, Norma Jean! Out. Out. OUT!

UTA. Yeah, take that greyhound bus terminal of yours to that creepy ex-playwright of yours who likes to have you piss on him!

NORMA JEAN. Well, up yours! I'm not going until I finish my drink!

GEORGIA. Oh, really. Well, we'll just see about that!

BARRY. (*Stopping* GEORGIA.) Hey, hey, come on—that's enough.

MONTGOMERY. Hey, come on, Barry—leave them alone. It's just getting good.

GEORGIA. I asked you to leave, Norma Jean.

UTA. We want you to go NOW!

NORMA JEAN. Well, now, let's see what the men think. Men: what do you think? Should I go, or should I just finish this little old drink here?

BARRY. Norma Jean, I mean, maybe . . .

MONTGOMERY. Hey, wait, hey man! I think she should stay! I mean, you're bad, Norma Jean, but I think you should most definitely stay. I mean, none of us is perfect, right man? (*Pause.*) I mean, we all make mistakes, right man? Right, Barry?

BARRY. Listen, faggot—why don't you relax, okay?

MONTGOMERY. What'd you call me?

UTA. He was only kidding.

MONTGOMERY. No, he wasn't—goddammit!

UTA. Well, don't scream at me!

GEORGIA. Please, everybody . . .

MONTGOMERY. You son-of-a-bitch. You dirty bastard. (*He lunges at* BARRY.) I'll kill you! (BARRY *picks up bar stool to protect himself. Girls scream—*UTA *gets in the way of the two men.*)

GEORGIA. Stop it! Stop it, all of you! What the hell is wrong with all of you? This is a party—my party! THIS IS A PARTY!

NORMA JEAN. (*Putting down her drink.*) Well, sweetheart—it looks like the party is over. (*She gathers her things. Crosses to the door as the two guys relax.*) Let's see now, how was my closing speech supposed to go. Oh, yes! (*As an actress.*) Georgia? Barry? Montgomery? Uta? I loved being here tonight. A night like this has always been a very rare thing in my life. That's why, I suppose, that I can safely and honestly say that tonight was the loveliest night of my life, simply because of the love of the four of you. (*She opens door.*) Goodbye. (*She's gone.*)

GEORGIA. (*Pause.*) Barry . . . Montgomery, are you all right?

BARRY. Just make me a drink. I'll stay right where I am, if somebody makes me a new drink. (*Dead silence.*)

GEORGIA. (*Finally.*) Well . . .

BARRY. It's three o'clock in the morning . . .

MONTGOMERY. We know . . .

UTA. We've already been through that . . .

GEORGIA. Is anybody hungry?

BARRY. No way.

MONTGOMERY. I'm fine. What about you, Uta? Are you hungry? (UTA *doesn't answer him.*)

GEORGIA. If I ate anything right now it would make me deathly sick.

BARRY. Then you're not going to eat anything now.

MONTGOMERY. What are you thinking of, Uta?

UTA. Oh, I don't know. I guess I was just thinking. Thinking about anything, *anything,* in order to keep from crying! Oh, God: do I feel like crying right now!

GEORGIA. You and me both, darling. (*A pause.*) You'd think we were all married or something: fighting like this.

UTA. Married . . . ? I never wanted to be married, but I have always wanted to have a baby. It's nice you're having this baby, Georgia. None of us really said it. But it's nice. I would love to have twins! A boy-twin and a girl-twin! I would love to spend the rest of my life bringing them up. I think that would be wonderful . . . (*A pause.*) I think I'll be going now.

MONTGOMERY. Do you want to come to my place for the rest of the night, Uta? It's not much of a place, but it's still a place, no matter how you look at it. You know what I mean? It's cozy and warm and really lived-in! God, is it *really* lived-in! You'd think a whole family lived in it. But there's only me. You know what I mean? Lots of plants too. Every afternoon at a certain time, because of the rays of the sun, you can actually believe that you're in a greenhouse or underneath a garden vineyard. It only lasts about thirty minutes, but it's still long enough. You know what I mean?

UTA. Oh, I know what you mean. And it all sounds just like a dream come true. But that's the whole point: it's just like a dream come true. It's not right, really. Why can't it all be just simply *real,* period?! Something that's *real,* that's also *true?!*

MONTGOMERY. I really just want you to come home with me tonight, Uta.

UTA. Like I was saying before, Montgomery: it all sounds just like a dream come true. But I'm not interested in dreams coming true. I figured it all out tonight: there's no way but the *real* way, *not* the dream way. Do you know what I mean, Montgomery? I mean: let's face it: if I go back to your apartment—which sounds so wonderful, by the way—if I go back there with you: well, we'd be faking it worse than we ever faked it before. You'd try to please me and I would try to please you, but we'd always be trying, we wouldn't really be doing it: we really wouldn't be pleasing each other at all. I mean, It wouldn't be natural, and it wouldn't be cozy, and it wouldn't be easy . . . it would be *unreal!* Totally unreal! I can't deal with that, Montgomery, and do you want to know something else?! You couldn't deal with it either! Let's try to deal with it on our own first, okay? It's the only way . . . ! (*A pause.*) I'm sorry, everybody. (*She starts to leave.*) Goodnight. I'll be in touch, I swear I will: Georgia . . . Barry . . . Montgomery . . . ? Goodnight again . . . (UTA *exits.*)

MONTGOMERY. I hated this goddam party! I hated it more than anything else I ever hated before in my whole life! And I hate myself for coming here!

GEORGIA. (*After a pause.*) I don't know what to say . . .

MONTGOMERY. You said enough, Queen Bee! Enough! I'm going too! I'm really pissed, Queen Bee! Uta shouldn't have listened to you! She should have listened to me! We could have tried, you know?! Uta and myself! We could have tried to get it on together, and off together! We really could have, you know?! I really bugged at you, Queen Bee!

GEORGIA. I'm sorry . . .

MONTGOMERY. It's too late now!

GEORGIA. It's never too late: that's my whole point, Montgomery.

MONTGOMERY. You just think you know everything: that's your whole problem. Well, I don't think you know as much as you think you know. I think you're just as fucked-up as the rest of us are fucked-up. You come on like this mother of us all. Big Mother Earth! Shit, that's all I can say! You made Uta leave all by herself. She could have gone home with me. But no: you had to open your big mouth. Who do you think you are, Georgia?! Some high priestess or something?! Do you know what?! I just thought about it! Maybe I like being a porno star, after all! Maybe we all do, after all! Maybe you're really just plain full of phony shit, Georgia! Deep down inside you probably know that there's nothing else that you can probably do better than what you do before the porno cameras on the porno screens. Uta shouldn't have listened to you! None of us should have listened to you! (MONTGOMERY *goes to the door.*) I'm glad you're having this baby, Georgia. Now maybe you'll stop treating us like babies . . . ! (MONTGOMERY *exits. A short pause.*)

BARRY. (*Finally.*) He's right.

GEORGIA. He's very young.

BARRY. Yeah. But he's still right.

GEORGIA. Look, darling: I've heard it from Norma Jean, I've heard it from Montgomery, and so I don't need to hear it from you. Not at this time, not under my roof. This is still my party.

BARRY. Yeah, well, speaking of your party: it was a real drag! And speaking of your roof: well, this fucking place of yours: it's like an ice-cube! It's cold and it's not cozy at all! It's like being on an operating table! It's like being in a morgue somewhere!

GEORGIA. Well, it may not have that lived-in look, darling, but at least it's not filled with monkeys and monkey shit!

BARRY. I'll take my place anyday! It might be full of monkey shit and it might not have much light and it might resemble a dungeon or a jail cell, but at least it's real! The smells are real and my monkey and his shit are real and I'm real, too! I mean, who do you think you are, Georgia?! Telling me to get rid of my pet monkey?! What about you?! Did I ever tell you to get rid of your five husbands?! You did it on your own, which, when you really think about it, well, it doesn't say too much for you, baby! Five husbands and miscarriages all over the place! That's a real turn-off, Georgia!

GEORGIA. It's none of your business!

BARRY. It is too! Because you've made it my business! Otherwise, don't broadcast so much about yourself all of the time, you understand?! Just don't think you got all of the answers all of the time, that's all. Because you don't have all of the answers! You're not perfect, no way! And by the way! Before I forget it! I'd like to know something! I'd like to know whose kid this is you're having! Yeah! I mean: you may think you have all of the answers! But what about that answer?! Who's the father of the kid?! Tell me that!

GEORGIA. You bastard! I think maybe you should leave! Right now!

BARRY. You haven't answered my question!

GEORGIA. Who the hell do you think you are?!

BARRY. I'm *me!* And me doesn't take any shit!

GEORGIA. You're just too cool to be good! Maybe you're just too cool to be true!

BARRY. What are you talking about?!

GEORGIA. Oh, your attitude! It's so "into yourself." The way you talk, and dress, the way you just "hang around" sometimes! You're like a Christmas tree ornament! You think you're the star on top of the Christmas tree! Someday, well, someday very soon: I can just see you outsmarting yourself, I can see you out-cooling yourself right out of your egomaniac pants! It's none of your business whose kid it is! I really could cry right now, I really could, but I'm not. I'm going to be so cool, even cooler than you could ever be. After all, you were my best teacher.

BARRY. Hey, Georgia: you want to know what I think . . . ?

GEORGIA. No.

BARRY. What I feel . . . ?

GEORGIA. No.

BARRY. I really think and feel that we're both cool, I really do. I mean, you didn't learn anything from me and I didn't learn anything from you. We're both pretty much cut out of the same cloth. We know each other too well because we're both so much alike.

GEORGIA. Oh, are we really?!

BARRY. I don't know about you: but I've always concentrated on being cool because deep down inside I didn't think I was cool at all. Listen, Georgia: I'm really just a simple person, not too complicated, or anything else like that. I'm sorry if I give the wrong impression. I'm just a guy who's trying like hell to get through everyday, even if it looks as though nothing ever bugs me at all. Everything bugs me at one time or another! Baby, all I do all of the time is to try and not be scared anymore, that's all! Nice guys are all over the place! I don't know what they're like! All I know is that I wanted to be accepted as much as possible by everybody, and so, it looked as though I was this extra-cool, extra-nice guy! Well, it's not true, Georgia! I'm a fucking raging volcanic mountain top deep down inside of me! And that's also why I'm so scared! (*A pause.*) And I'm getting older too . . . just like you. And that doesn't make me feel too good, either. Georgia: I just want something to hang onto, before it's too late. I really think that that's what you're all about too, I really do. Aren't you? (*A pause.*) *Aren't you?!* (GEORGIA *remains silent; she does not move. Eventually,* BARRY *gets ready to leave and heads for the door.*)

GEORGIA. Where are you going, Barry?

BARRY. (*Turning to face her.*) I'm leaving. I'm tired. Tired of being mothered by you. I don't want a mother. And I don't want a nurse, either, Clara Barton. I want more than that. I want something real! I want something that's really real!

GEORGIA. (*After a pause.*) Like Lorna Lou . . . ?

BARRY. (*Another pause.*) Lorna Lou . . . ? That's another sick trip, baby.

GEORGIA. Wanna tell me about it?

BARRY. Well, it's like this, see? You know . . . we've never made love yet . . . my girlfriend Lorna Lou and me. It's a game we've always played. You know how much I like foreplay?! I just love foreplay. I love it almost more than I love actual balling, except for when you're coming, that is. But even that's a gyp in the end because it doesn't last long enough: *coming.* (*A pause.*) I once asked this Irish poet who I met in some Irish bar one time, I said to him: "Why does coming last for such a short time?" He smiled at me, and then he finally said back to me: "Believe me, son, it lasts long enough, *coming*. If it lasted longer than it already does, well, you just couldn't take it, you just simply couldn't stand it. If it lasted twenty or thirty minutes like you just mentioned to me, son, well, you would go out of your mind for good, or maybe you'd even die." (*A pause.*) Oh, Georgia, you know how great I am before the cameras?! It's been so hard in *real* life! That's why foreplay really turns me on. When do we ever get to act out foreplay in our films together?! (*A pause.*) Nobody wants that. They pay five bucks to see the action, baby. You know that! They pay five bucks for a dream. (*A silence.*)

GEORGIA. (*Finally.*) Hey, Barry: little-boy-wonder: do you want something that's real? (*A pause.*) Remember that *one* time, Barry, not too long ago, darling, when the two of us were both standing there stark naked, facing each other, in that cold windy old barn that was filled with drafts over on Staten Island? There we were, Barry, a little less than three months ago, in fact, before the cameras for the thirteenth time together, and all of a sudden those horny cameras began to grind away, and then, before we knew it, we were grinding away like we had never grinded away before, remember that chilly afternoon, darling? Well, we weren't so chilly, were we, now? We were hot, hotter than we had ever been before, remember? We were so hot that we never listened to our director, did we now? He kept saying, "All right, now take it out now! Take it out! Show it all to the audience! The audience wants to see it! That's what they pay all that money for in all of those movie houses! Pull it out, Barry, pull it out, for Christ's sake!" (*A pause.*) But Barry never pulled it out, did he? And Georgia here was really glad that he never pulled it out . . . because she loved Barry. And Barry was really glad that he never pulled it out, either, because it looked as though Barry was in love with Georgia too. (*A pause.*) Remember, Barry . . . ? (BARRY *stares at* GEORGIA.)

BARRY. You mean . . . ?

GEORGIA. Yes.
BARRY. You mean that your baby . . . ?
GEORGIA. Yes.
BARRY. You mean that your baby is also gonna be my baby?
GEORGIA. Yes.
BARRY. You know something? I think we've made history. Medical history. Spiritual history. Our baby was conceived on film, did you ever think of that, Georgia? What a trip! (BARRY *gives* GEORGIA *a long, loving look.*)

BARRY. (*Finally.*) I love you. (GEORGIA *smiles at* BARRY, *and then she picks up a pillow and throws it at him: hitting him in the face.*) Now what did you go and do that for?

GEORGIA. (*A pause.*) That is what is known as a beginning part of *foreplay*.

BLACKOUT

CURTAIN

THE END

MUSIC USE NOTE

Licensees are solely responsible for obtaining formal written permission from copyright owners to use copyrighted music in the performance of this play and are strongly cautioned to do so. If no such permission is obtained by the licensee, then the licensee must use only original music that the licensee owns and controls. Licensees are solely responsible and liable for all music clearances and shall indemnify the copyright owners of the play(s) and their licensing agent, Samuel French, against any costs, expenses, losses and liabilities arising from the use of music by licensees. Please contact the appropriate music licensing authority in your territory for the rights to any incidental music.

IMPORTANT BILLING AND CREDIT REQUIREMENTS

If you have obtained performance rights to this title, please refer to your licensing agreement for important billing and credit requirements.

www.ingramcontent.com/pod-product-compliance
Lightning Source LLC
Chambersburg PA
CBHW072020290426
44109CB00018B/2297